# Mometrix TEST PREPARATION



# PSSA

## Grade 6 English Language Arts Success Strategies

# Dear Future Exam Success Story

First of all, **THANK YOU** for purchasing Mometrix study materials!

Second, congratulations! You are one of the few determined test-takers who are committed to doing whatever it takes to excel on your exam. **You have come to the right place.** We developed these study materials with one goal in mind: to deliver you the information you need in a format that's concise and easy to use.

In addition to optimizing your guide for the content of the test, we've outlined our recommended steps for breaking down the preparation process into small, attainable goals so you can make sure you stay on track.

We've also analyzed the entire test-taking process, identifying the most common pitfalls and showing how you can overcome them and be ready for any curveball the test throws you.

Standardized testing is one of the biggest obstacles on your road to success, which only increases the importance of doing well in the high-pressure, high-stakes environment of test day. Your results on this test could have a significant impact on your future, and this guide provides the information and practical advice to help you achieve your full potential on test day.

**Your success is our success**

**We would love to hear from you!** If you would like to share the story of your exam success or if you have any questions or comments in regard to our products, please contact us at **800-673-8175** or **support@mometrix.com**.

Thanks again for your business and we wish you continued success!

Sincerely,
The Mometrix Test Preparation Team


Written and edited by the Mometrix Test Preparation Team
Printed in the United States of America

# Table of Contents

# Introduction

**Thank you for purchasing this resource**! You have made the choice to prepare yourself for a test that could have a huge impact on your future, and this guide is designed to help you be fully ready for test day. Obviously, it's important to have a solid understanding of the test material, but you also need to be prepared for the unique environment and stressors of the test, so that you can perform to the best of your abilities.

For this purpose, the first section that appears in this guide is the **Success Strategies**. We've devoted countless hours to meticulously researching what works and what doesn't, and we've boiled down our findings to the most impactful steps you can take to improve your performance on the test. We start at the beginning with study planning and move through the preparation process, all the way to the testing strategies that will help you get the most out of what you know when you're finally sitting in front of the test.

We recommend that you start preparing for your test as far in advance as possible. However, if you've bought this guide as a last-minute study resource and only have a few days before your test, we recommend that you skip over the first two Success Strategies since they address a long-term study plan.

If you struggle with **test anxiety**, we strongly encourage you to check out our recommendations for how you can overcome it. Test anxiety is a formidable foe, but it can be beaten, and we want to make sure you have the tools you need to defeat it.

# Strategy #1 – Plan Big, Study Small

There's a lot riding on your performance. If you want to ace this test, you're going to need to keep your skills sharp and the material fresh in your mind. You need a plan that lets you review everything you need to know while still fitting in your schedule. We'll break this strategy down into three categories.

## Information Organization

Start with the information you already have: the official test outline. From this, you can make a complete list of all the concepts you need to cover before the test. Organize these concepts into groups that can be studied together, and create a list of any related vocabulary you need to learn so you can brush up on any difficult terms. You'll want to keep this vocabulary list handy once you actually start studying since you may need to add to it along the way.

## Time Management

Once you have your set of study concepts, decide how to spread them out over the time you have left before the test. Break your study plan into small, clear goals so you have a manageable task for each day and know exactly what you're doing. Then just focus on one small step at a time. When you manage your time this way, you don't need to spend hours at a time studying. Studying a small block of content for a short period each day helps you retain information better and avoid stressing over how much you have left to do. You can relax knowing that you have a plan to cover everything in time. In order for this strategy to be effective though, you have to start studying early and stick to your schedule. Avoid the exhaustion and futility that comes from last-minute cramming!

## Study Environment

The environment you study in has a big impact on your learning. Studying in a coffee shop, while probably more enjoyable, is not likely to be as fruitful as studying in a quiet room. It's important to keep distractions to a minimum. You're only planning to study for a short block of time, so make the most of it. Don't pause to check your phone or get up to find a snack. It's also important to **avoid multitasking**. Research has consistently shown that multitasking will make your studying dramatically less effective. Your study area should also be comfortable and well-lit so you don't have the distraction of straining your eyes or sitting on an uncomfortable chair.

The time of day you study is also important. You want to be rested and alert. Don't wait until just before bedtime. Study when you'll be most likely to comprehend and remember. Even better, if you know what time of day your test will be, set that time aside for study. That way your brain will be used to working on that subject at that specific time and you'll have a better chance of recalling information.

Finally, it can be helpful to team up with others who are studying for the same test. Your actual studying should be done in as isolated an environment as possible, but the work of organizing the information and setting up the study plan can be divided up. In between study sessions, you can discuss with your teammates the concepts that you're all studying and quiz each other on the details. Just be sure that your teammates are as serious about the test as you are. If you find that your study time is being replaced with social time, you might need to find a new team.

# Strategy #2 – Make Your Studying Count

You're devoting a lot of time and effort to preparing for this test, so you want to be absolutely certain it will pay off. This means doing more than just reading the content and hoping you can remember it on test day. It's important to make every minute of study count. There are two main areas you can focus on to make your studying count.

## Retention

It doesn't matter how much time you study if you can't remember the material. You need to make sure you are retaining the concepts. To check your retention of the information you're learning, try recalling it at later times with minimal prompting. Try carrying around flashcards and glance at one or two from time to time or ask a friend who's also studying for the test to quiz you.

To enhance your retention, look for ways to put the information into practice so that you can apply it rather than simply recalling it. If you're using the information in practical ways, it will be much easier to remember. Similarly, it helps to solidify a concept in your mind if you're not only reading it to yourself but also explaining it to someone else. Ask a friend to let you teach them about a concept you're a little shaky on (or speak aloud to an imaginary audience if necessary). As you try to summarize, define, give examples, and answer your friend's questions, you'll understand the concepts better and they will stay with you longer. Finally, step back for a big picture view and ask yourself how each piece of information fits with the whole subject. When you link the different concepts together and see them working together as a whole, it's easier to remember the individual components.

Finally, practice showing your work on any multi-step problems, even if you're just studying. Writing out each step you take to solve a problem will help solidify the process in your mind, and you'll be more likely to remember it during the test.

## Modality

*Modality* simply refers to the means or method by which you study. Choosing a study modality that fits your own individual learning style is crucial. No two people learn best in exactly the same way, so it's important to know your strengths and use them to your advantage.

For example, if you learn best by visualization, focus on visualizing a concept in your mind and draw an image or a diagram. Try color-coding your notes, illustrating them, or creating symbols that will trigger your mind to recall a learned concept. If you learn best by hearing or discussing information, find a study partner who learns the same way or read aloud to yourself. Think about how to put the information in your own words. Imagine that you are giving a lecture on the topic and record yourself so you can listen to it later.

For any learning style, flashcards can be helpful. Organize the information so you can take advantage of spare moments to review. Underline key words or phrases. Use different colors for different categories. Mnemonic devices (such as creating a short list in which every item starts with the same letter) can also help with retention. Find what works best for you and use it to store the information in your mind most effectively and easily.

# Strategy #3 – Practice the Right Way

Your success on test day depends not only on how many hours you put into preparing, but also on whether you prepared the right way. It's good to check along the way to see if your studying is paying off. One of the most effective ways to do this is by taking practice tests to evaluate your progress. Practice tests are useful because they show exactly where you need to improve. Every time you take a practice test, pay special attention to these three groups of questions:

- The questions you got wrong
- The questions you had to guess on, even if you guessed right
- The questions you found difficult or slow to work through

This will show you exactly what your weak areas are, and where you need to devote more study time. Ask yourself why each of these questions gave you trouble. Was it because you didn't understand the material? Was it because you didn't remember the vocabulary? Do you need more repetitions on this type of question to build speed and confidence? Dig into those questions and figure out how you can strengthen your weak areas as you go back to review the material.

Additionally, many practice tests have a section explaining the answer choices. It can be tempting to read the explanation and think that you now have a good understanding of the concept. However, an explanation likely only covers part of the question's broader context. Even if the explanation makes perfect sense, **go back and investigate** every concept related to the question until you're positive you have a thorough understanding.

As you go along, keep in mind that the practice test is just that: practice. Memorizing these questions and answers will not be very helpful on the actual test because it is unlikely to have any of the same exact questions. If you only know the right answers to the sample questions, you won't be prepared for the real thing. **Study the concepts** until you understand them fully, and then you'll be able to answer any question that shows up on the test.

It's important to wait on the practice tests until you're ready. If you take a test on your first day of study, you may be overwhelmed by the amount of material covered and how much you need to learn. Work up to it gradually.

On test day, you'll need to be prepared for answering questions, managing your time, and using the test-taking strategies you've learned. It's a lot to balance, like a mental marathon that will have a big impact on your future. Like training for a marathon, you'll need to start slowly and work your way up. When test day arrives, you'll be ready.

Start with the strategies you've read in the first two Success Strategies—plan your course and study in the way that works best for you. If you have time, consider using multiple study resources to get different approaches to the same concepts. It can be helpful to see difficult concepts from more than one angle. Then find a good source for practice tests. Many times, the test website will suggest potential study resources or provide sample tests.

## Practice Test Strategy

If you're able to find at least three practice tests, we recommend this strategy:

### UNTIMED AND OPEN-BOOK PRACTICE

Take the first test with no time constraints and with your notes and study guide handy. Take your time and focus on applying the strategies you've learned.

### TIMED AND OPEN-BOOK PRACTICE

Take the second practice test open-book as well, but set a timer and practice pacing yourself to finish in time.

### TIMED AND CLOSED-BOOK PRACTICE

Take any other practice tests as if it were test day. Set a timer and put away your study materials. Sit at a table or desk in a quiet room, imagine yourself at the testing center, and answer questions as quickly and accurately as possible.

Keep repeating timed and closed-book tests on a regular basis until you run out of practice tests or it's time for the actual test. Your mind will be ready for the schedule and stress of test day, and you'll be able to focus on recalling the material you've learned.

# Strategy #4 – Pace Yourself

Once you're fully prepared for the material on the test, your biggest challenge on test day will be managing your time. Just knowing that the clock is ticking can make you panic even if you have plenty of time left. Work on pacing yourself so you can build confidence against the time constraints of the exam. Pacing is a difficult skill to master, especially in a high-pressure environment, so **practice is vital**.

Set time expectations for your pace based on how much time is available. For example, if a section has 60 questions and the time limit is 30 minutes, you know you have to average 30 seconds or less per question in order to answer them all. Although 30 seconds is the hard limit, set 25 seconds per question as your goal, so you reserve extra time to spend on harder questions. When you budget extra time for the harder questions, you no longer have any reason to stress when those questions take longer to answer.

Don't let this time expectation distract you from working through the test at a calm, steady pace, but keep it in mind so you don't spend too much time on any one question. Recognize that taking extra time on one question you don't understand may keep you from answering two that you do understand later in the test. If your time limit for a question is up and you're still not sure of the answer, mark it and move on, and come back to it later if the time and the test format allow. If the testing format doesn't allow you to return to earlier questions, just make an educated guess; then put it out of your mind and move on.

On the easier questions, be careful not to rush. It may seem wise to hurry through them so you have more time for the challenging ones, but it's not worth missing one if you know the concept and just didn't take the time to read the question fully. Work efficiently but make sure you understand the question and have looked at all of the answer choices, since more than one may seem right at first.

Even if you're paying attention to the time, you may find yourself a little behind at some point. You should speed up to get back on track, but do so wisely. Don't panic; just take a few seconds less on each question until you're caught up. Don't guess without thinking, but do look through the answer choices and eliminate any you know are wrong. If you can get down to two choices, it is often worthwhile to guess from those. Once you've chosen an answer, move on and don't dwell on any that you skipped or had to hurry through. If a question was taking too long, chances are it was one of the harder ones, so you weren't as likely to get it right anyway.

On the other hand, if you find yourself getting ahead of schedule, it may be beneficial to slow down a little. The more quickly you work, the more likely you are to make a careless mistake that will affect your score. You've budgeted time for each question, so don't be afraid to spend that time. Practice an efficient but careful pace to get the most out of the time you have.

# Test-Taking Strategies

This section contains a list of test-taking strategies that you may find helpful as you work through the test. By taking what you know and applying logical thought, you can maximize your chances of answering any question correctly!

It is very important to realize that every question is different and every person is different: no single strategy will work on every question, and no single strategy will work for every person. That's why we've included all of them here, so you can try them out and determine which ones work best for different types of questions and which ones work best for you.

## Question Strategies

### ✓ READ CAREFULLY

Read the question and the answer choices carefully. Don't miss the question because you misread the terms. You have plenty of time to read each question thoroughly and make sure you understand what is being asked. Yet a happy medium must be attained, so don't waste too much time. You must read carefully and efficiently.

### ✓ CONTEXTUAL CLUES

Look for contextual clues. If the question includes a word you are not familiar with, look at the immediate context for some indication of what the word might mean. Contextual clues can often give you all the information you need to decipher the meaning of an unfamiliar word. Even if you can't determine the meaning, you may be able to narrow down the possibilities enough to make a solid guess at the answer to the question.

### ✓ PREFIXES

If you're having trouble with a word in the question or answer choices, try dissecting it. Take advantage of every clue that the word might include. Prefixes can be a huge help. Usually, they allow you to determine a basic meaning. *Pre-* means before, *post-* means after, *pro-* is positive, *de-* is negative. From prefixes, you can get an idea of the general meaning of the word and try to put it into context.

### ✓ HEDGE WORDS

Watch out for critical hedge words, such as *likely, may, can, often, almost, mostly, usually, generally, rarely,* and *sometimes*. Question writers insert these hedge phrases to cover every possibility. Often an answer choice will be wrong simply because it leaves no room for exception. Be on guard for answer choices that have definitive words such as *exactly* and *always*.

### ✓ SWITCHBACK WORDS

Stay alert for *switchbacks*. These are the words and phrases frequently used to alert you to shifts in thought. The most common switchback words are *but, although,* and *however*. Others include *nevertheless, on the other hand, even though, while, in spite of, despite,* and *regardless of*. Switchback words are important to catch because they can change the direction of the question or an answer choice.

### ⊘ FACE VALUE

When in doubt, use common sense. Accept the situation in the problem at face value. Don't read too much into it. These problems will not require you to make wild assumptions. If you have to go beyond creativity and warp time or space in order to have an answer choice fit the question, then you should move on and consider the other answer choices. These are normal problems rooted in reality. The applicable relationship or explanation may not be readily apparent, but it is there for you to figure out. Use your common sense to interpret anything that isn't clear.

## Answer Choice Strategies

### ⊘ ANSWER SELECTION

The most thorough way to pick an answer choice is to identify and eliminate wrong answers until only one is left, then confirm it is the correct answer. Sometimes an answer choice may immediately seem right, but be careful. The test writers will usually put more than one reasonable answer choice on each question, so take a second to read all of them and make sure that the other choices are not equally obvious. As long as you have time left, it is better to read every answer choice than to pick the first one that looks right without checking the others.

### ⊘ ANSWER CHOICE FAMILIES

An answer choice family consists of two (in rare cases, three) answer choices that are very similar in construction and cannot all be true at the same time. If you see two answer choices that are direct opposites or parallels, one of them is usually the correct answer. For instance, if one answer choice says that quantity *x* increases and another either says that quantity *x* decreases (opposite) or says that quantity *y* increases (parallel), then those answer choices would fall into the same family. An answer choice that doesn't match the construction of the answer choice family is more likely to be incorrect. Most questions will not have answer choice families, but when they do appear, you should be prepared to recognize them.

### ⊘ ELIMINATE ANSWERS

Eliminate answer choices as soon as you realize they are wrong, but make sure you consider all possibilities. If you are eliminating answer choices and realize that the last one you are left with is also wrong, don't panic. Start over and consider each choice again. There may be something you missed the first time that you will realize on the second pass.

### ⊘ AVOID FACT TRAPS

Don't be distracted by an answer choice that is factually true but doesn't answer the question. You are looking for the choice that answers the question. Stay focused on what the question is asking for so you don't accidentally pick an answer that is true but incorrect. Always go back to the question and make sure the answer choice you've selected actually answers the question and is not merely a true statement.

### ⊘ EXTREME STATEMENTS

In general, you should avoid answers that put forth extreme actions as standard practice or proclaim controversial ideas as established fact. An answer choice that states the "process should be used in certain situations, if..." is much more likely to be correct than one that states the "process should be discontinued completely." The first is a calm rational statement and doesn't even make a definitive, uncompromising stance, using a hedge word *if* to provide wiggle room, whereas the second choice is far more extreme.

### ⊘ BENCHMARK

As you read through the answer choices and you come across one that seems to answer the question well, mentally select that answer choice. This is not your final answer, but it's the one that will help you evaluate the other answer choices. The one that you selected is your benchmark or standard for judging each of the other answer choices. Every other answer choice must be compared to your benchmark. That choice is correct until proven otherwise by another answer choice beating it. If you find a better answer, then that one becomes your new benchmark. Once you've decided that no other choice answers the question as well as your benchmark, you have your final answer.

### ⊘ PREDICT THE ANSWER

Before you even start looking at the answer choices, it is often best to try to predict the answer. When you come up with the answer on your own, it is easier to avoid distractions and traps because you will know exactly what to look for. The right answer choice is unlikely to be word-for-word what you came up with, but it should be a close match. Even if you are confident that you have the right answer, you should still take the time to read each option before moving on.

## General Strategies

### ⊘ TOUGH QUESTIONS

If you are stumped on a problem or it appears too hard or too difficult, don't waste time. Move on! Remember though, if you can quickly check for obviously incorrect answer choices, your chances of guessing correctly are greatly improved. Before you completely give up, at least try to knock out a couple of possible answers. Eliminate what you can and then guess at the remaining answer choices before moving on.

### ⊘ CHECK YOUR WORK

Since you will probably not know every term listed and the answer to every question, it is important that you get credit for the ones that you do know. Don't miss any questions through careless mistakes. If at all possible, try to take a second to look back over your answer selection and make sure you've selected the correct answer choice and haven't made a costly careless mistake (such as marking an answer choice that you didn't mean to mark). This quick double check should more than pay for itself in caught mistakes for the time it costs.

### ⊘ PACE YOURSELF

It's easy to be overwhelmed when you're looking at a page full of questions; your mind is confused and full of random thoughts, and the clock is ticking down faster than you would like. Calm down and maintain the pace that you have set for yourself. Especially as you get down to the last few minutes of the test, don't let the small numbers on the clock make you panic. As long as you are on track by monitoring your pace, you are guaranteed to have time for each question.

### ⊘ DON'T RUSH

It is very easy to make errors when you are in a hurry. Maintaining a fast pace in answering questions is pointless if it makes you miss questions that you would have gotten right otherwise. Test writers like to include distracting information and wrong answers that seem right. Taking a little extra time to avoid careless mistakes can make all the difference in your test score. Find a pace that allows you to be confident in the answers that you select.

### ⊘ Keep Moving

Panicking will not help you pass the test, so do your best to stay calm and keep moving. Taking deep breaths and going through the answer elimination steps you practiced can help to break through a stress barrier and keep your pace.

## Final Notes

The combination of a solid foundation of content knowledge and the confidence that comes from practicing your plan for applying that knowledge is the key to maximizing your performance on test day. As your foundation of content knowledge is built up and strengthened, you'll find that the strategies included in this chapter become more and more effective in helping you quickly sift through the distractions and traps of the test to isolate the correct answer.

Now that you're preparing to move forward into the test content chapters of this book, be sure to keep your goal in mind. As you read, think about how you will be able to apply this information on the test. If you've already seen sample questions for the test and you have an idea of the question format and style, try to come up with questions of your own that you can answer based on what you're reading. This will give you valuable practice applying your knowledge in the same ways you can expect to on test day.

**Good luck and good studying!**

# English Language Arts

## The Writing Process

### Brainstorming

When choosing what to write about, activities like brainstorming can help inspire new ideas or help writers see how their ideas go together. **Brainstorming** means considering a variety of topics or ideas and is mainly used to find a creative approach to a subject or problem. A good first step in brainstorming is simple **free-association** with a topic. One way of doing this is sitting down with paper and pen and writing every thought that comes to mind about the topic in a word or phrase. It does not matter how helpful or good the thought seems at first; the writer should write down everything that comes to mind about the topic. Then, the writer should read the list over a few times. Next, he or she should look for patterns, repetitions, and clusters of ideas. This allows a variety of fresh ideas to come as the writer thinks about the topic.

### Free Writing

Free writing is a more organized form of brainstorming. **Free writing** means taking a limited amount of time, like 2 to 3 minutes, to write everything that comes to mind about a topic in complete sentences. When the time is up, the writer should review everything he or she has written down. Many of the sentences may not make sense, but they may contain ideas and details that help the writer organize his or her ideas and prepare to plan the composition. Usually, free writing results in more useful ideas than brainstorming because the writer's thoughts and connections are written in complete sentences. However, both methods can be used together to help the writer prepare to plan and write a composition.

### Mapping

One specific way to use graphic organizers is to map an essay. There are many different types of graphic organizers. One easy method to create one is to draw a circle in the middle of the page and write a broad topic in it. Then, draw smaller circles with related topics and ideas, or with topics that fit within the broad topic, written inside and draw line to connect each circle to the main circle. This method can show ideas that fit within the broad topic and will help guide the essay, or it can show which ideas may work better as the main topic of the essay.

Once the main idea and other ideas and details for the essay have been chosen, they can be used to map the essay. Mapping is another word for using a certain type of graphic organizer. These graphic organizers look like a map and organize ideas and details as they will appear in the essay. The essay map can have the main idea at the top or in the center. If the main idea is at the top, the supporting ideas will appear below it in a row, and any additional details will appear under the supporting idea they go with. If the main idea appears in the center, the supporting ideas may appear around it, and the additional details will appear around the supporting ideas they go with.

### Planning

Planning is the process of organizing a piece of writing before writing a draft. At the beginning of planning, writers should decide **why they are writing** and **who will read what they write**. The writer must also choose a **genre**, which is the **type** of composition he or she will write. There are fiction genres, such as comedy, folklore, action, and mystery. There are also nonfiction genres, such as essays, reports, poems, and journals. To plan his or her composition, a writer may create an outline or a graphic organizer, such as a Venn diagram, a spider-map, or a flowchart. These methods should help the writer choose their topic, main ideas, and how to organize the composition. If the writer needs to do research for the composition, he or she may also do so as they plan. Planning helps writers organize all of their ideas and decide if they have enough information to begin their first draft. However, writers should remember that the decisions they make during planning may change later, so their plan does not have to be perfect.

## DRAFTING

Writers may then use their plan, outline, or graphic organizer to compose their first draft. They may write more drafts after the first one to improve their writing. Writing multiple drafts can help writers think of different ways to state their ideas and correct mistakes that may be hard to fix without rewriting a section of the composition, or the whole composition. There is no "right" number of drafts, so different writers may write a different number of drafts. Writing drafts also makes it easier to write freely because a writer can improve his or her composition with each draft they write.

## REVISING, EDITING, AND PROOFREADING

Once a writer completes a draft, he or she can move on to revising, editing, and proofreading to improve the draft. **Revising** is making sure that the composition is right for the audience, is not missing important information, is on topic, and is well organized. The writer should also consider the composition's style when revising and ensure that it is appropriately formal or serious. Revising may happen after the first draft so that errors are not repeated in the next draft. Each draft should be revised before the next one is written so that no mistakes are missed. **Editing** comes next. Editing a composition includes steps like improving transitions between paragraphs and making sure each paragraph is on topic. While editing, the writer must pay attention to the words he or she uses and the way the information in each paragraph is organized. Writers may also fix grammar mistakes in the editing phase, since some errors will require a writer to rewrite large parts of their work. **Proofreading** means fixing misspelled words, errors in grammar, and any other small mistakes in the composition.

During the revising, editing, and proofreading steps, it can be helpful for writers to ask a peer to read their work, since he or she may notice mistakes or problems the writer missed before. A writer may also choose to read his or her own work aloud, or listen to someone else read it. Hearing a composition aloud can help writers find mistakes or opportunities for improvement in their work more easily. This happens because when something is read aloud, the person reading the text must pay closer attention to the words on the page. When a writer or a peer reads the composition, they should point out any sentence that confuses them the first time they read it. Most of these sentences can be revised in a way that makes it easier to read and understand.

### *ADDING AND REMOVING INFORMATION*

While both revising and editing may involve changing the words in a composition, they can also involve adding or taking away words. When a writer has completed a draft and reread it, he or she may notice that something, such as a transition, important details, or an explanatory sentence, is missing. Simply changing the words to make the passage sound better will not solve this problem, so the writer must **add** whatever words and information is needed to make the passage make sense and achieve the writer's purpose.

In other cases, a writer may have words, a sentence, or sometimes an entire paragraph that gives unnecessary information or explains the information in a way that is confusing. When this happens, the extra words and information weaken the composition and must be **removed**. Sometimes, this is difficult for writers to do because it may require them to remove writing they are proud of or a fact they find interesting. Despite this, revising and editing are steps meant to improve and strengthen a composition, so the writer should change, add, or remove parts of his or her writing in a way that makes it better and achieves his or her purpose.

### *Revising Sentences*

**Sentence variety** is important to consider when writing an essay. A variety of sentence lengths and types can make an essay more engaging, and different types of sentences can sometimes help readers better understand information. For example, a sentence containing a list may make more sense when written with a simple sentence structure, since writing a compound sentence containing a list may give the reader too much information at once. On the other hand, information that is closely related and can be connected with a conjunction should be written in a compound sentence, rather than a simple sentence, since a compound sentence helps the reader see that the information goes together.

Using only simple sentences often makes writing boring and bothersome to read. Writing using only compound sentences makes it difficult for writers to explain information well and difficult for readers to understand, since every sentence will include a coordinating conjunction. To check an essay for sentence variety, it is helpful to look at whether the essay contains different sentence structures and lengths. It is also important to pay attention to the way each sentence starts and avoid beginning with the same words or phrases.

### *Revising Vocabulary*

When writing informational or argumentative texts, it is important to use **precise vocabulary**, or **word choice**, to explain your main idea and supporting details. Generalized vocabulary will not help the audience fully understand the points that you are attempting to make because it will not accurately explain your main idea and supporting details. Precise vocabulary is important to use because it will accurately describe the ideas that are central to your text. When you research a subject, make sure to familiarize yourself with any vocabulary that is involved in its explanation. Use context clues, dictionaries, or, if necessary, a technical dictionary to decode any words that you are not familiar with. Precise vocabulary also impacts the effectiveness of narrative text. Carefully choosing vocabulary to describe sensory details, or imagery, helps writers paint the best possible picture of the events they are describing through their writing.

## Recursive Writing Process

Brainstorming, planning, drafting, revising, editing, and proofreading are all steps in the **writing process**. This process is helpful to remember when beginning a new composition, but once a writer has practiced these steps in this order, he or she can use the **recursive writing process**. The recursive writing process is the same as the normal writing process, but the steps in the recursive writing process do not have to happen in the same order. For example, one writer may need to repeat steps after completing other steps. A different writer may discover that he or she can practice the planning and revising steps as he or she writes a draft. The recursive writing process involves moving back and forth between planning, drafting, and revising, followed by more planning, more drafting, and more revising until the writer is happy with his or her work. Each writer can use the recursive writing process in their own way, as long as it helps them improve their work and write the best they can.

**Review Video: Recursive Writing Process**
Visit mometrix.com/academy and enter code: 951611

# Essay Structure and Organization

## Central Ideas and Supporting Details

In the first paragraph of a composition, writers include a sentence that explains the **central idea.** This sentence is also known as the **thesis**. The rest of the paragraph shows the reader why the topic of the essay is interesting and includes details that support the central idea. One way to understand the relationship between the central idea and supporting information is to think about a table: the tabletop is the central idea, and each of the table's legs is a supporting detail or group of details. All of the legs work together to support the tabletop and create a table, just like the supporting details work together to support the central idea and create a composition.

## Introduction

The introduction is used to capture the reader's attention and announce the essay's central idea. Normally, the introduction contains about 3-5 sentences. An introduction can begin with an interesting quote, a question, a strong opinion, or something else that will **interest** the reader's and prompt them to keep reading. If the composition has a prompt, the introduction should **restate** or **summarize** some part of the prompt so that the reader will have an idea of what information will be in the essay. Finally, your introduction should include the **central idea**, the primary thing the essay will tell the reader.

**Review Video: Introduction**
Visit mometrix.com/academy and enter code: 961328

## Body

In an essay's introduction, the writer states the central idea and prepares the reader for the information in the rest of the composition. In the body of the composition, the writer **explains**, **demonstrates**, and **gives more information about** the **central idea**. This is done using supporting details and examples that are relevant to the central idea of the composition. For example, if the composition's central idea is a vacation the writer took, the body will include descriptions of where the writer went, what they experienced, and what they thought of the trip. If the composition's central idea is the writer's opinion, the body will include examples and facts that show why he or she has formed that opinion. If composition's central idea is a topic and the writer wants to instruct the reader, the body will contain facts, explanations, and examples that help teach the reader about the central idea. A writer will use supporting details to explain the central idea throughout the body.

The body should also contain multiple paragraphs, and the order the writer puts these paragraphs in is important. Each paragraph should include at least one supporting detail, but a paragraph may include more than one if two or more supporting details work together to support the central idea. If the central idea is to describe something that happened, the paragraphs should match the order in which the events occurred. If the central idea is to present an opinion or instruct the reader, the paragraphs should be ordered in the way that would make the most sense to the reader. The order of body paragraphs is important because it can impact how easy a composition is to read.

**Review Video: Drafting Body Paragraphs**
Visit mometrix.com/academy and enter code: 724590

## Choosing Supporting Details and Examples

When writing an informative or argumentative text, writers must choose supporting details carefully. Including details that are irrelevant, inaccurate, or vague does not strengthen the author's writing, while relevant, accurate, provable, and specific details do strengthen the author's writing. These details can make the writer's meaning clearer or give evidence that the author's points are true or logical. Such details may include examples or facts, such as statistics, statements from others who have authority on the subject, and common events or experiences. Choosing appropriate supporting details can also help the author show that they put effort into forming their ideas. This can also make the composition more intriguing and enjoyable to read, since the writer's own interest and insight will be apparent to the reader.

## PARAGRAPHS

After the introduction of a passage, the body paragraphs will explain and elaborate upon the central idea. While each paragraph should relate to the central idea of the composition, each paragraph should focus on one point or supporting detail. Normally, a paragraph has a good topic sentence that summarizes the paragraph's main point. A topic sentence is a sentence that gives an introduction to the paragraph and its contents. Topic sentences should contain information that is more specific than what is in the introduction and may include a supporting detail, but they should not contain explanations or examples.

The next sentences in the paragraph should support the topic sentence. These sentences can contain examples, explanations, or other specific information that supports the topic sentence, which supports the central idea of the composition. While a paragraph may be structured in any way, as long as it logically provides information that supports the central idea, it can be best to use a template or pattern to make sure that each paragraph is complete and well organized. For example, a good template to follow is topic sentence, evidence, explanation, conclusion. This means that after the topic sentence, the next sentence should provide evidence, like a quote or example, that supports the paragraph's main point. Next, the paragraph should include a sentence that explains how that evidence supports the paragraph's main point. If there are multiple examples or quotes, more than one sentence may be used to explain them. Finally, there should be a concluding sentence that helps the reader understand the paragraph and prepares them for the next one.

A paragraph must contain enough information to support its main point and the composition's central idea. A paragraph of two or three sentences will most likely not support the main point or central idea because it is not likely to contain enough information, explanation, or evidence. When a paragraph does not support the main point or central idea, it does not help the writer achieve their purpose or goal for writing the essay. A helpful, informative paragraph will often have somewhere from three to five sentences. Also, it is important that the sentences within the paragraph lead the reader through the information. Each paragraph should flow logically and stay on topic throughout.

### *STARTING A NEW PARAGRAPH*

For most forms of writing, you will need to use multiple paragraphs. This means that deciding when to start a new paragraph is very important. Reasons for starting a new paragraph include:

- To separate the introduction and conclusion from the body paragraphs
- To move from one supporting detail or point to another
- To indicate an important shift in time or place
- To show a comparison, contrast, or cause and effect relationship

## TRANSITIONS

Transitions between sentences and paragraphs guide readers from idea to idea and show relationships between sentences and paragraphs. Writers should use transitions carefully and only when they are truly helpful. They should also be selected to fit the author's purpose. Transitions can show relationships such as time, comparison, an order of events, and cause and effect. Transitions are often used at the beginning of a phrase, sentence, or paragraph, since this helps prepare the reader for the next piece of information.

**Review Video: Transitions in Writing**
Visit mometrix.com/academy and enter code: 233246

### Types of Transitional Words

| | |
|---|---|
| **Time** | Afterward, immediately, earlier, meanwhile, recently, lately, now, since, soon, when, then, until, before, etc. |
| **Sequence** | too, first, second, further, moreover, also, again, and, next, still, besides, finally |
| **Comparison** | similarly, in the same way, likewise, also, again, once more |
| **Contrasting** | but, although, despite, however, instead, nevertheless, on the one hand... on the other hand, regardless, yet, in contrast. |
| **Cause and Effect** | because, consequently, thus, therefore, then, to this end, since, so, as a result, if... then, accordingly |
| **Examples** | for example, for instance, such as, to illustrate, indeed, in fact, specifically |
| **Place** | near, far, here, there, to the left/right, next to, above, below, beyond, opposite, beside |
| **Repetition, Summary, or Conclusion** | as mentioned earlier, as noted, in other words, in short, on the whole, to summarize, therefore, as a result, to conclude, in conclusion |
| **Addition** | and, also, furthermore, moreover |

**Review Video: Transition Words**
Visit mometrix.com/academy and enter code: 707563

### Conclusion

The conclusion of a composition should summarize the central idea and show that it has been explained well. A good conclusion shows the reader why the author's central idea is meaningful and important and how the supporting details should help the reader understand the central idea. The conclusion should also give the reader something to think about that is related to the central idea. For example, in the conclusion, the author can invite readers to think about how they feel or what they think after reading the composition. Some things to avoid when writing conclusions include:

- Introducing a completely new idea
- Apologizing for one's opinions or writing
- Repeating the central idea word for word rather than summarizing them
- Using the conclusion to summarize every detail in the composition

**Review Video: Drafting Conclusions**
Visit mometrix.com/academy and enter code: 209408

# Grammar

## SUBJECTS AND PREDICATES

### *SUBJECTS*

Every sentence needs a subject and a predicate. The **subject** of a sentence names who or what the sentence is about. The subject may be directly stated in a sentence, or the subject may be implied. The **complete subject** includes the simple subject and any **modifiers**, such as adjectives, articles, prepositions, and adverbs, that go with it. To find the complete subject, ask *Who* or *What* before the verb to complete the question. The answer, including any modifiers, is the complete subject. To find the **simple subject**, remove all of the modifiers in the complete subject.

Examples:

simple subject
The small, red car is the one that he wants for Christmas.
complete subject

simple subject
The young artist is coming over for dinner.
complete subject

**Review Video: Subjects in English**
Visit mometrix.com/academy and enter code: 444771

An imperative sentence is a sentence that gives someone instructions or makes a request to someone. In **imperative** sentences, the verb's subject is understood, but is not actually present in the sentence. For example, this about the sentence *Drive to the store*. This sentence is a command, and the subject is *you*. If the subject were directly stated, the sentence would be *You, drive to the store*. Another fact to consider is that, normally, the subject comes before the verb. However, the subject comes after the verb in sentences that begin with *There are* or *There was*.

Direct:

| | | |
|---|---|---|
| John knows the way to the park. | Who knows the way to the park? | John |
| The cookies need ten more minutes. | What needs ten minutes? | The cookies |
| By five o'clock, Bill will need to leave. | Who needs to leave? | Bill |
| There are five letters on the table for him. | What is on the table? | Five letters |
| There were coffee and doughnuts in the house. | What was in the house? | Coffee and doughnuts |

Implied:

| | | |
|---|---|---|
| Go to the post office for me. | Who is going to the post office? | You |
| Come and sit with me, please? | Who needs to come and sit? | You |

### *Predicates*

In a sentence, there is always a predicate and a subject. The subject tells what the sentence is about, and the **predicate** explains or describes the subject.

Think about the sentence *He sings*. In this sentence, we have a subject, *He*, and a predicate, *sings*. This is all that is needed for a sentence to be complete. Most sentences contain more information, but if this is all the information that is given in a sentence, then it is a complete sentence.

Now, let's look at another sentence: *John and Jane sing on Tuesday nights at the dance hall.*

subject: John and Jane — predicate: sing on Tuesday nights at the dance hall.

John and Jane sing on Tuesday nights at the dance hall.

## Subject-Verb Agreement

Verbs **agree** with their subjects in number. In other words, singular subjects need singular verbs. Plural subjects need plural verbs. **Singular** is for **one** person, place, or thing. **Plural** is for **more than one** person, place, or thing. Subjects and verbs must also share the same point of view, as in first, second, or third person.

**Review Video: Subject-Verb Agreement**
Visit mometrix.com/academy and enter code: 479190

### *Number Agreement Examples:*

Single Subject and Verb: Dan (singular subject) calls (singular verb) home.

Dan is one person. So, the singular verb *calls* is needed.

Plural Subject and Verb: Dan and Bob (plural subject) call (plural verb) home.

More than one person needs the plural verb *call*.

### *Person Agreement Examples:*

First Person: I *am* walking.

Second Person: You *are* walking.

Third Person: He *is* walking.

## Complications with Subject-Verb Agreement

### *Words Between Subject and Verb*

Words that come between the simple subject and the verb do not affect subject-verb agreement.

Examples:

The joy (singular subject) of my life returns (singular verb) home tonight.

The phrase *of my life* does not affect the verb *returns*.

singular subject / singular verb

The question that still remains unanswered is "Who are you?"

Don't let the phrase "*that still remains…*" confuse you. The subject *question* goes with the verb *is*.

### Compound Subjects

A compound subject is formed when two or more nouns joined by *and*, *or*, or *nor* act together as the subject of the sentence.

#### Joined by And

When a compound subject is joined by *and*, it is treated as a plural subject and requires a plural verb.

Examples:

plural subject / plural verb

You and Jon are invited to come to my house.

plural subject / plural verb

The pencil and paper belong to me.

#### Joined by Or/Nor

For a compound subject joined by *or* or *nor*, the verb must agree in number with the part of the subject that is closest to the verb.

Examples:

subject / verb

Today or tomorrow is the day.

subject / verb

Stan or Phil wants to read the book.

subject / verb

Neither the pen nor the book is on the desk.

subject / verb

Either the blanket or pillows arrive this afternoon.

### Indefinite Pronouns as Subject

An indefinite pronoun is a pronoun that does not refer to a specific noun. Different indefinite pronouns are used as a singular noun, a plural noun, or change depending on how they are used.

#### Always Singular

Pronouns such as *each*, *either*, *everybody*, *anybody*, *somebody*, and *nobody* are always singular. This is because these pronouns always stand in for one person, place, or thing.

Examples:

singular subject — singular verb

Each of the runners has a different bib number.

singular verb — singular subject

Is either of you ready for the game?

Note: The words *each* and *either* can also be used as adjectives. For example, *each* person is unique. When one of these adjectives modifies the subject of a sentence, it is always a singular subject.

singular subject — singular verb

Everybody grows a day older every day.

singular subject — singular verb

Anybody is welcome to bring a tent.

#### Always Plural

Pronouns such as *both*, *several*, and *many* are always plural. This is because these pronouns always stand in for more than one person, place, thing, or idea.

Examples:

plural subject — plural verb

Both of the siblings were too tired to argue.

plural subject — plural verb

Many have tried, but none have succeeded.

#### Depend on Context

Pronouns such as *some*, *any*, *all*, *none*, *more*, and *most* can be either singular or plural depending on what they are representing in the context of the sentence.

Examples:

singular subject — singular verb

All of my dog's food was still there in his bowl.

plural subject — plural verb

By the end of the night, all of my guests were already excited about coming to my next party.

### *Other Cases Involving Plural or Irregular Form*

Some nouns are **singular in meaning but plural in form**: news, mathematics, physics, and economics.

The *news is* coming on now.

*Mathematics is* my favorite class.

Some nouns are plural in form and meaning, and have **no singular equivalent**: scissors and pants.

Do these *pants come* with a shirt?

The *scissors are* for my project.

Note: Look to your **dictionary** for help when you aren't sure whether a noun with a plural form has a singular or plural meaning.

#### *Example*

**Which word should go in the blank?**

If Kelly is going to the party, Joan and Susan ____ going to the store.

a. Is
b. Are
c. Am
d. Was

Try using each choice in the sentence. Choice A, *is*, forms this sentence: If Kelly is going to the party, Joan and Susan is going to the store. There are two people, Joan and Susan, who are going to the store. This makes the subject of the clause plural. *Is* is a singular verb, meaning it does not agree with the subject and cannot be the answer.

Choice B, *are*, forms this sentence: If Kelly is going to the party, Joan and Susan are going to the store. The subject of the clause is still plural. But *are* is a plural verb! The subject and verb agree, so *are* is the correct answer.

Choice C, *am*, forms this sentence: If Kelly is going to the party, Joan and Susan am going to the store. *Am* is a singular verb, and it is also only used in first person, when the writer or speaker is referring to themself. The subject of the clause is plural, and the sentence is in third person, so *am* is not the correct answer.

Choice D, *was*, forms this sentence: If Kelly is going to the party, Joan and Susan was going to the store. *Was* is a singular verb, so it does not agree with the plural subject in this clause.

### Complements

A complement is a noun, pronoun, or adjective that is used to give more information about the subject or verb in the sentence.

#### *Direct Objects*

A direct object is a noun or pronoun that takes or receives the **action** of a verb. A complete sentence does not need a direct object, so not all sentences will have them. When you are looking for a direct object, find the verb and ask *who* or *what*.

Examples:

I took *the blanket.*

Jane read *books.*

#### *Indirect Objects*

An indirect object is a word or group of words that show how an action had an **influence** on someone or something. If there is an indirect object in a sentence, then you always have a direct object in the sentence. When you are looking for the indirect object, find the verb and ask *to*, *for*, *whom*, or *what*.

Examples:

We taught [the old dog]<sub></sub>

We taught the old dog (indirect object) a new trick (direct object).

I gave them (indirect object) a math lesson (direct object).

**Review Video: Direct and Indirect Objects**
Visit mometrix.com/academy and enter code: 817385

## PHRASES

A phrase is a group of words that functions as a single part of speech, usually a noun, adjective, or adverb. A **phrase** is not a complete thought, and does not contain a subject, but it adds detail or explanation to a sentence, or renames something within the sentence.

## CLAUSES

A clause is a group of words that contains both a subject and a predicate (verb). There are two types of clauses: independent and dependent. An **independent clause** contains a complete thought, while a **dependent (or subordinate) clause** does not. A dependent clause includes a subject and a verb, and may also contain additional information, but it cannot stand as a complete thought without being joined to an independent clause. Dependent clauses function within sentences as adjectives, adverbs, or nouns.

Example:

I am running (independent clause) because I want to stay in shape (dependent clause).

The clause *I am running* is an independent clause: it has a subject and a verb, and it gives a complete thought. The clause *because I want to stay in shape* is a dependent clause: it has a subject and a verb, but it does not express a complete thought. This is due to the fact that it begins with *because*, which shows that there is more information needed to complete the thought. This dependent clause adds detail to the independent clause to which it is attached.

**Review Video: Independent and Dependent Clauses**
Visit mometrix.com/academy and enter code: 556903

## SENTENCE STRUCTURE

Sentence structure is based on the type and number of clauses in the sentence. Two common sentence structures are simple sentences and compound sentences:

**Simple**: A simple sentence has one independent clause with no dependent clauses. A simple sentence may have a **compound subject** or a **compound verb**, or both.

Examples:

single subject / single verb
Judy watered the lawn.

compound subject / single verb
Judy and Alan watered the lawn.

single subject / compound verb / compound verb
Judy watered the lawn and pulled weeds.

compound subject / compound verb / compound verb
Judy and Alan watered the lawn and pulled weeds.

**Compound**: A compound sentence has two or more independent clauses with no dependent clauses. Usually, the independent clauses are joined with a comma and a coordinating conjunction or with a semicolon.

Examples:

independent clause / independent clause
The time has come, and we are ready.

independent clause / independent clause
I woke up at dawn; the sun was just coming up.

**Complex**: A complex sentence has one independent clause and at least one dependent clause.

Examples:

dependent clause / independent clause
Although he had the flu, Harry went to work.

independent clause / dependent clause
Marcia got married after she finished college.

**Review Video: Sentence Structure**
Visit mometrix.com/academy and enter code: 700478

## Sentence Fragments

Recall that a group of words must contain at least one **independent clause** in order to be considered a sentence. If it doesn't contain even one independent clause, it is called a **sentence fragment**.

Choosing the best steps for **repairing** a sentence fragment depends on what type of fragment it is. If the fragment is a dependent clause, it can sometimes be fixed by simply removing a subordinating word, such as *when*, *because*, or *if*, from the beginning of the fragment. Alternatively, a dependent clause can be joined to a closely related neighboring sentence. If the fragment is missing some required part, like a subject or a verb, it may be fixed by simply adding the missing part.

Examples:

**Fragment**: Because he wanted to sail the Mediterranean.

**Removed subordinating word**: He wanted to sail the Mediterranean.

**Combined with another sentence**: Because he wanted to sail the Mediterranean, he booked a Greek island cruise.

### EXAMPLE

**Which of the following changes will NOT correct this sentence fragment?**

Although she had found the coin first.

a. Remove *Although.*
b. Add a comma and *she let her brother keep it* after *first.*
c. Add *She let her brother keep the coin* before *although.*
d. Remove *first.*

Choice A suggests removing the word *although* to form the following sentence: She found the coin first. This option removes the subordinating conjunction to make the clause independent. The resulting sentence is complete, so removing *although* is an acceptable way to correct the fragment. Choice A is incorrect.

Choice B forms the following sentence: Although she had found the coin first, she let her brother keep it. A comma and an independent clause have been added to the sentence fragment to form a complex sentence. The resulting sentence is complete and written correctly, so choice B is incorrect.

Choice C forms the following sentence: She let her brother keep the coin although she had found the coin first. An independent clause has been added before the sentence fragment to form a complex sentence. This sentence is correctly written and complete, so choice C is an acceptable way to correct the fragment. Choice C is incorrect.

Choice D removes the word *first*, leaving *Although she had found the coin*. This is still a sentence fragment, since it is a single dependent clause. Choice D does not correct the fragment, so D is correct.

## RUN-ON SENTENCES

Run-on sentences consist of multiple independent clauses that have not been joined together properly. Run-on sentences can be corrected in several different ways:

**Join clauses properly**: This can be done with a comma and coordinating conjunction, with a semicolon, or with a colon or dash if the second clause is explaining something in the first clause.

Example:

**Incorrect**: I went on the trip, we visited lots of castles.

**Corrected**: I went on the trip, and we visited lots of castles.

**Split into separate sentences**: This correction is best to use when the independent clauses are very long or when they are not closely related.

Example:

**Incorrect**: The drive to New York takes ten hours, my uncle lives in Boston.

**Corrected**: The drive to New York takes ten hours. My uncle lives in Boston.

**Make one clause dependent**: This is the easiest way to make the sentence correct and more interesting at the same time. It's often as simple as adding a subordinating word between the two clauses or before the first clause.

Example:

**Incorrect**: I finally made it to the store and I bought some eggs.

**Corrected**: When I finally made it to the store, I bought some eggs.

**Reduce to one clause with a compound verb**: If both clauses have the same subject, remove the subject from the second clause, and you now have just one clause with a compound verb.

Example:

**Incorrect**: The drive to New York takes ten hours, it makes me very tired.

**Corrected**: The drive to New York takes ten hours and makes me very tired.

Note: While these are the simplest ways to correct a run-on sentence, often the best way is to completely reorganize the thoughts in the sentence and rewrite it.

### *COMMA SPLICES*

A comma splice is a specific error that may appear in a run-on sentence. When a sentence has two independent clauses, but the clauses are joined with only a comma, a **comma splice** is formed. Remember that if two independent clauses are joined with a comma, a coordinating conjunction is also needed. Most of the solutions for fixing run-on sentences can also be used to correct a comma splice.

**Review Video: Fragments and Run-on Sentences**
Visit mometrix.com/academy and enter code: 541989

### *EXAMPLE*

Rick wants to go see a movie tomorrow he would miss his sister's recital.

**Identify the change that would NOT correct this run-on sentence.**

a. Add a comma after *tomorrow*.
b. Split it into two sentences between *tomorrow* and *he*.
c. Add a comma and *but* after *tomorrow*.
d. Add a subordinating conjunction to make one of the clauses dependent.

Choice A says to add a comma after *tomorrow*. This forms the following sentence: Rick wants to go see a movie tomorrow, he would miss his sister's recital. A comma has been used to join two independent clauses, but there is no coordinating conjunction. This choice forms a comma splice, so it is not an acceptable correction for this sentence. Choice A is the correct answer.

Choice B says to split the sentence into two sentences. This forms the following two sentences: Rick wants to go see a movie tomorrow. He would miss his sister's recital. Both of these sentences are complete. This is an acceptable way to correct the run-on sentence, so choice B is incorrect.

Choice C says to add a coordinating conjunction after *tomorrow*. This forms the following sentence: Rick wants to go see a movie tomorrow, but he would miss his sister's recital. A comma and a coordinating conjunction have been added between the two independent clauses. This is an acceptable way to correct a run-on sentence. Choice C is incorrect.

Choice D says to add a subordinating conjunction to make one of the sentences dependent. There are many new sentences that could be created by adding a subordinating conjunction. For example, consider the following sentence: Although Rick wants to go see a movie tomorrow, he would miss his sister's recital. Alternatively, the following sentence could also be created: Rick wants to go see a movie tomorrow even though he would miss his sister's recital. Both of these sentences have an independent clause and a dependent clause. These sentences are both complete and written correctly, so choice D is incorrect.

### *EXAMPLE*

**Identify the sentence that has a comma splice.**

a. Tom stopped at the store to buy supplies and his family met him at the campsite.
b. The ball rolled into the living room quietly, but it still startled the dog.
c. Theresa brought her mom some flowers, her mom did not have a vase.
d. Sweet potatoes, pecans, and brown sugar are all ingredients in my cousin's sweet potato casserole.

Choice A has two independent clauses joined by a coordinating conjunction. This is incorrect because there should be a comma before the coordinating conjunction. While the sentence is written incorrectly, there is no comma, so this sentence does not have a comma splice. Choice A is incorrect.

Choice B has two independent clauses joined by a comma and a coordinating conjunction. This is the correct way to write a compound sentence, so there is no error here. Choice B is incorrect.

Choice C has two independent clauses joined by a comma. This is incorrect because independent clauses should be joined together by a comma and a coordinating conjunction. When the comma is present without a coordinating conjunction between two independent clauses, a comma splice is formed. This means that choice C is correct.

Choice D is a simple sentence that contains one independent clause. The only commas used in this sentence are used to separate items in a list. There are no clauses that need to be joined or errors related to commas, so choice D does not contain a comma splice. Choice D is incorrect.

## THE EIGHT PARTS OF SPEECH

### *NOUNS*

When you talk about a person, place, thing, or idea, you are talking about a **noun**. The two main types of nouns are **common** and **proper** nouns.

### Common Nouns

**Common nouns** are generic names for people, places, and things. Common nouns are not usually capitalized.

Examples of common nouns:

*People*: boy, girl, worker, manager

*Places*: school, bank, library, home

*Things*: dog, cat, truck, car

### Proper Nouns

**Proper nouns** name specific people, places, or things. All proper nouns are capitalized.

Examples of proper nouns:

*People*: Abraham Lincoln, George Washington, Martin Luther King, Jr.

*Places*: Los Angeles, California; New York; Asia

*Things*: Statue of Liberty, Earth, Lincoln Memorial

Note: When referring to the planet that we live on, capitalize *Earth*. When referring to the dirt, rocks, or land, lowercase *earth*.

### Singular and Plural Nouns

**Singular nouns** name **one** person, place, thing, or idea. **Plural nouns** name **more than one** person, place, thing, or idea. Most nouns have both a singular and plural form. Many plural nouns are spelled like the singular noun with an *-s* at the end, but this is not true for all plural nouns. Singular nouns that already end in an *s*, *o*, *ch*, *sh*, or *x* usually end in *-es* when they are in the plural form. Singular nouns that end in a consonant followed by the letter *y* will usually lose the *y* and end in *-ies* in the plural form, and words that end with the letter *f* or *fe* will usually lose the *f* and end in *-ves*.

Some plural nouns have much different spellings than their singular form, and some plural nouns are spelled the same as their singular form. There are more rules for spelling plural nouns, but these are the most common spelling changes.

Examples of singular nouns:

Typical nouns: dog, pencil, girl, store, hope, stingray

Nouns ending in *s*, *o*, *ch*, *sh*, or *x*: mass, hero, lunch, polish, fox

Nouns ending in a consonant and *y*: puppy, baby, fairy, sky

Nouns ending in *f* or *fe*: self, life, calf, hoof

Examples of plural nouns:

Typical nouns: dogs, pencils, girls, stores, hopes, stingrays

Nouns ending in *s*, *o*, *ch*, *sh*, or *x*: masses, heroes, lunches, polishes, foxes

Nouns ending in a consonant and *y*: puppies, babies, fairies, skies

Nouns ending in a vowel and *f* or *fe*: selves, lives, calves, hooves

### Collective Nouns

**Collective nouns** are the names for a group of people, places, or things that function like singular nouns. The following are examples of collective nouns: *class, company, dozen, group, herd, team,* and *public*. Collective nouns usually require an article, such as *a*, *an*, and *the*, which shows that the noun is a single unit. For example, a choir is a group of singers. Even though there are many singers in a choir, the word choir describes a single group. If we refer to the members of the group, and not the group itself, it is no longer a collective noun.

Incorrect: The *choir are* going to compete nationally this year.

Correct: The *choir is* going to compete nationally this year.

Incorrect: The *members* of the choir *is* competing nationally this year.

Correct: The *members* of the choir *are* competing nationally this year.

## Pronouns

Pronouns are words that are used to stand in for nouns. There are several different types of pronouns, but the two main types are subjective and objective pronouns. **Subjective** nouns and pronouns that those that are the subject of a sentence. **Objective** nouns and pronouns are those that are an object in a sentence. Another important type of pronoun is the personal pronoun, which refers to people. Personal pronouns can be subjective or objective. **Possessive** nouns and pronouns show possession or ownership. Pronouns can also be singular or plural.

*Singular*

| Subjective | Objective | Possessive |
|---|---|---|
| I | Me | My, Mine |
| You | You | Your, Yours |
| He | Him | His |
| She | Her | Her, hers |
| It | It | Its |
| Who | Whom | Whose |

*Plural*

| Subjective | Objective | Possessive |
|---|---|---|
| we | us | our, ours |
| you | you | your, yours |
| they | them | their, theirs |

**Reflexive**: Reflexive pronouns are pronouns that function as the object of a sentence and refer to the subject. Examples of reflexive pronouns include *myself, yourself, himself, herself, itself, ourselves, yourselves*, and *themselves*.

**Indefinite**: Indefinite pronouns are used to refer to multiple nouns or an undefined noun. Examples of indefinite nouns include *all, any, each, everyone, either/neither, one, some*, and *several*.

**Relative**: Relative pronouns are used to connect relative clauses that specify or describe a noun to the rest of the sentence. Examples of relative pronouns include *which, who, whom,* and *whose.*

**Review Video: Nouns and Pronouns**
Visit mometrix.com/academy and enter code: 312073

### EXAMPLE

**Which of the following sentences uses a relative pronoun?**

a. My mother is the person who baked the chocolate cake.
b. Who is in charge of choosing decorations for the party?
c. She is the only person from my hometown to win an Olympic medal.
d. Which car broke down this week?

Remember that a relative pronoun is one that appears at or near the beginning of a relative clause and links the clause to the rest of the sentence. Interrogative pronouns are pronouns that are used to begin a question. Some pronouns, like *who, which, whom,* and *whose,* can be either interrogative or relative pronouns, depending on how they are used in a sentence, so it is important to pay attention how these words are used in each answer choice.

What is the pronoun in choice A? This sentence includes the word *who,* which can be a relative pronoun. What function does this pronoun have in the sentence? The sentence begins with *my mother is the person*. Which person? *Who* links the relative clause, *who baked the chocolate cake,* to this independent clause and specifies which person the speaker's mother is. That means that *who* is a relative pronoun in this sentence, and choice A is correct.

What is the pronoun in choice B? The first word is *who,* which we know can be a relative pronoun. However, in this sentence, *who* is the first word. It signals the beginning of a question. It does not connect a relative clause to the rest of the sentence. *Who* is an interrogative pronoun in this sentence, so choice B is incorrect.

What is the pronoun in choice C? There is only one pronoun, *my,* which cannot be a relative pronoun. While this sentence could easily be rewritten to include a relative pronoun and clause, it does not include either. Choice C is incorrect.

What is the pronoun in choice D? The first word is *which,* which can be used as either an interrogative or a relative pronoun. *Which* is the first word in this sentence, though. It is not used to link a relative clause that describes or specifies a noun. *Which* is used as an interrogative pronoun in this sentence, so choice D is incorrect.

## *VERBS*

If you want to write a sentence, then you need a verb. Without a verb, you have no sentence. The verb of a sentence indicates action or being. In other words, the verb shows something's action or state of being or the action that has been done to something.

### ACTION VERBS AND LINKING VERBS

**Action verbs** show what the subject is doing. In other words, an action verb shows action. **Linking verbs** link the subject of a sentence to a noun or pronoun. They can also link a subject to an adjective, so the linking verb helps create a description. You always need a verb if you want a complete sentence. However, linking verbs on their own cannot be a complete sentence. Any verb that shows a condition and connects to a noun, pronoun, or adjective that describes the subject of a sentence is a linking verb.

**Action**: He sings. | Run! | Go! | I talk with him every day. | She reads.

**Linking**:

Incorrect: I am.

Correct: I am John. | I smell roses. | I feel tired.

> **Review Video: Action Verbs and Linking Verbs**
> Visit mometrix.com/academy and enter code: 743142

### Verb Tenses

A verb **tense** shows the different form of a verb to point to the time of an action. The present and past tense are indicated by the verb's form. An action in the present, *I talk,* can change form for the past: *I talked*. However, for future tense, an auxiliary, or helping, verb is sometimes needed to show the change in form. When writing a composition, it is important to use verb tenses consistently. Choose the best tense for the composition and do not switch to a different tense unless it is necessary or appropriate for a particular sentence or paragraph.

Present: I talk
Past: I talked
Future: I will talk

**Present**: The action happens at the current time.

Example: He *walks* to the store every morning.

**Past**: The action happened in the past.

Example: He *walked* to the store an hour ago.

**Future**: The action is going to happen later.

Example: I *will walk* to the store tomorrow.

> **Review Video: Verb Tenses**
> Visit mometrix.com/academy and enter code: 269472

### Irregular Verbs

While most verbs gain the suffix -ed when used in the past tense, irregular verbs receive different spelling changes when they are written in the past tense. For example, *walk* is a regular verb, and it becomes *walked* when written in the past tense. However, *run* is an irregular verb because it becomes *ran* when written in the past tense.

EXAMPLE

My mother _____ me about the big nest of ants near the sandbox. I thanked her for telling me!

**Which of the following verbs should go in the blank?**

a. Warn
b. Warned
c. Will warn
d. Warns

First, look at the sentences. The first sentence does not have enough information to show which tense it is in. However, the second sentence says that the child thanked the mother. The verb here is *thanked*, which is the past-tense form of *thank*. Because the second sentence is in the past tense, it makes sense to say that the first sentence is also in past tense.

Choice A says that the missing verb is *warn. Warn* is a present-tense verb, but it can be used in the future tense if a helping verb is present. However, this sentence is in past tense, so it needs a past-tense verb. Choice A is wrong.

Choice B says that the missing verb is *warned. Warned* is a past-tense verb, and it logically completes the sentence. Choice B is correct!

Choice C says that the missing verb is *will warn. Will warn* is a future-tense verb, meaning that it describes an action that will occur in the future. However, since the speaker already thanked his or her mother for the warning, it is not logical to use a future-tense verb in the blank. Choice C is incorrect.

Choice D says that the missing verb is *warns. Warn* is usually used with plural subjects, and *warns* used with single subjects. *Warns* can be used in the future or present tense, but it cannot be used in the past tense. Since the sentence is in the past tense, it needs a past-tense verb, so D is incorrect.

### *ADJECTIVES*

An **adjective** is a word that is used to modify a noun or pronoun. An adjective answers a question: *Which one? What kind?* or *How many?* Usually, adjectives come before the words that they modify, but they may also come after a linking verb.

Which one? The *third* suit is my favorite.

What kind? This suit is *navy blue*.

How many? I am going to buy *four* pairs of socks to match the suit.

**Review Video: Descriptive Text**
Visit mometrix.com/academy and enter code: 174903

#### COMPARISON WITH ADJECTIVES

Some adjectives are relative, and other adjectives are absolute. Adjectives that are **relative** can show the comparison between things. **Absolute** adjectives can also show comparison, but they do so in a different way. Let's say that you are reading two books. You think that one book is perfect, and the other book is not exactly perfect. It is not possible for one book to be more perfect than the other. Either you think that the book is perfect, or you think that the book is imperfect. In this case, perfect and imperfect are absolute adjectives.

Relative adjectives will show the different **degrees** of something or someone to something else or someone else. The three degrees of adjectives include positive, comparative, and superlative.

The **positive** degree is the normal form of an adjective.

Example: This work is *difficult.* | She is *smart.*

The **comparative** degree compares one person or thing to another person or thing.

Example: This work is *more difficult* than your work. | She is *smarter* than me.

The **superlative** degree compares more than two people or things.

Example: This is the *most difficult* work of my life. | She is the *smartest* lady in school.

**Review Video: Adjectives**
Visit mometrix.com/academy and enter code: 470154

### *ADVERBS*

An **adverb** is a word that is used to **modify,** or describe, a verb, adjective, or another adverb. Usually, adverbs answer one of these questions: *When? Where? How?* and *Why?* The negatives *not* and *never* are considered adverbs. Adverbs that modify adjectives or other adverbs **strengthen** or **weaken** the words that they modify.

Examples:

He walks *quickly* through the crowd.

The water flows *smoothly* on the rocks.

Note: Adverbs are usually indicated by the suffix *-ly*, which has been added to the root word. For instance, *quick* can be made into an adverb by adding *-ly* to construct *quickly*. Some words that end in *-ly* do not follow this rule and can function as other parts of speech. Examples of adjectives ending in *-ly* include: *early, friendly, holy, lonely, silly*, and *ugly*. To know if a word that ends in *-ly* is an adjective or adverb, check your dictionary. Also, while many adverbs end in *-ly*, you need to remember that not all adverbs end in *-ly*.

Examples:

He is *never* angry.

You are *too* irresponsible to travel alone.

#### TYPES OF ADVERBS

Different types of adverbs are used to describe particular aspects of a verb, adjective, or other adverb. The following are examples of common types of adverbs:

**Time:** Some adverbs show when something was done, such as *yesterday*, *today*, or *in two days.*

**Manner:** Some adverbs show the way something was done, such as *hurriedly, neatly, grumpily*, or *loudly.*

**Frequency:** Some adverbs show how often something was done, such as *seldom*, *often*, *never*, or *often*.

**Degree:** Some adverbs show how much or to what degree something was done, such as *completely*, *barely*, *highly*, or *halfway*.

**Conjunctive:** Conjunctive adverbs are used similarly to conjunctions, as they connect different ideas, but they can connect ideas from different clauses or sentences. Some examples of conjunctive adverbs are *however*, *alternatively*, *likewise*, and *then*.

### Comparison with Adverbs

The rules for comparing adverbs are the same as the rules for adjectives.

The **positive** degree is the standard form of an adverb.

> Example: He arrives *soon*. | She speaks *softly* to her friends.

The **comparative** degree compares one person or thing to another person or thing.

> Example: He arrives *sooner* than Sarah. | She speaks *more softly* than him.

The **superlative** degree compares more than two people or things.

> Example: He arrives *soonest* of the group. | She speaks the *most softly* of any of her friends.

**Review Video: Adverbs**
Visit mometrix.com/academy and enter code: 713951

### Example

**Identify the conjunctive adverb in the following sentences.**

> Every night, Savannah's brother loudly gets up to get a glass of water. Consequently, she has started sleeping with earmuffs on so that he does not wake her up at night.

a. Every night
b. Loudly
c. Consequently
d. At night

Choice A says that *every night* is a conjunctive adverb. What does *every night* describe in this sentence? It describes how often Savannah's brother loudly gets a glass of water. This means that *every night* shows the frequency that Savannah's brother does this action. Since *every night* is an adverb that shows frequency, choice A is incorrect.

Choice B says that *loudly* is a conjunctive adverb. In this sentence, what does *loudly* describe? It describes the way that Savannah's brother gets a glass of water each night. This means that *loudly* is an adverb that shows manner. *Loudly* is not a conjunctive adverb, so choice B is incorrect.

Choice C says that *consequently* is a conjunctive adverb. What function does *consequently* have in this sentence? It shows the reason that Savannah started wearing earmuffs while she sleeps. It also shows a connection between the information in the first sentence and the information in the second sentence. Since *consequently* connects the ideas in these sentences, it is a conjunctive adverb. Choice C is correct.

Choice D says that *at night* is a conjunctive adverb. *At* and *night* work together to form an adverbial phrase. Which type of adverb do they form? In this sentence, *at night* shows when Savannah wants to avoid being woken up by her brother. This makes *at night* an adverb that shows time, meaning that *at night* is not a conjunctive adverb and choice D is incorrect.

### PREPOSITIONS

A **preposition** is a word placed before a noun or pronoun that shows the relationship between an object and another word in the sentence.

*Common prepositions*:

| | | | | |
|---|---|---|---|---|
| about | before | during | on | under |
| after | beneath | for | over | until |
| against | between | from | past | up |
| among | beyond | in | through | with |
| around | by | of | to | within |
| at | down | off | toward | without |

Examples:

The napkin is *in* the drawer.

The Earth rotates *around* the Sun.

The needle is *beneath* the haystack.

Can you find "me" *among* the words?

### PREPOSITIONAL PHRASES

One important thing to know about prepositions is that they form special phrases, called prepositional phrases. A **prepositional phrase** begins with a preposition and ends with a noun or pronoun that is the object of the preposition. Normally, the prepositional phrase functions as an **adjective** or an **adverb** within the sentence.

Examples:

The picnic is [on the blanket] (prepositional phrase).

I am sick [with a fever] (prepositional phrase) today.

[Among the many flowers,] (prepositional phrase) John found a four-leaf clover.

Be careful not to mistake the object in a prepositional phrase as the subject of a sentence. The subject of the sentence will not be found in a prepositional phrase because a prepositional phrase is used to describe how an object is related to the subject. Prepositional phrases do not influence subject-verb agreement.

**Review Video: Prepositions**
Visit mometrix.com/academy and enter code: 946763

EXAMPLE

**Which of the following could NOT complete the sentence?**

She went ____ the cave.

a. Sadly
b. Into
c. From
d. Through

Choice A says that the missing word is *sadly*. The blank is between *went* and *the cave*, meaning that the missing word will connect these pieces of the sentence. While *sadly* could be used here to show how the girl felt, there would still be missing information. A preposition is needed here to show whether she entered, exited, or stood outside of the cave. *Sadly* is an adverb, so A is the correct answer.

Choice B says that *into* would complete the sentence. Does *into* complete the sentence without leaving missing information? To say *she went into the cave* is a logical, complete sentence. Choice B is incorrect.

Choice C says that the missing word is *from*. This creates the sentence *she went from the cave*. Since she could have left the cave to go somewhere else, this is also a logical, complete sentence. Choice C is incorrect.

Choice D says that *through* would complete the sentence. The sentence would read *she went through the cave*. Since she could have explored the whole cave or found an exit on the other side of it, *through* can logically complete the sentence. Choice D is incorrect.

EXAMPLE

**Identify the prepositional phrase in the following sentence.**

Mable visited the store to buy some vegetables.

a. To buy
b. Visited the store
c. The store to buy
d. To buy some vegetables

Remember the pieces of a prepositional phrase. Prepositional phrases should begin with a preposition and end with a noun or pronoun. Considering these rules, can any of the answer choices be eliminated? Choice B and choice C can be eliminated because neither choice begins with a preposition!

That leaves choices A and D. Choice A says that the prepositional phrase is *to buy*. This does start with a preposition, and it does give more information about Mable's trip to the store. However, it does not end with a noun or pronoun. Choice D says that the prepositional phrase is *to buy some vegetables*. Choice D begins with a preposition and ends with a noun, and it explains why Mabel went to the store.

Choice D is the only choice that has all of the pieces of a prepositional phrase, so D is correct!

### Example

Read the sentence below and answer the following question.

A band with 15 members _____ performing at my restaurant tonight.

**Identify the verb that best completes the sentence.**

a. Were
b. Is
c. Are
d. Are not

This question is asking which verb should go in the blank. There are a couple of reasons why choosing the correct verb for this sentence may be confusing. First of all, there are two nouns that appear before the verb. Second, one of these nouns is singular and one is plural.

The first step is to determine which noun goes with the verb. The two nouns are *band* and *members*. While *members* is closest to the blank, it is part of a prepositional phrase that describes *band*. The subject of the sentence is *band*, so the verb must agree with *band*.

Is *band* singular or plural? The sentence says that the band has multiple members, but there is only one band. *Band* is a collective noun, meaning that it is a singular noun. This means that the correct verb will also be singular. With this in mind, can any of the answer choices be eliminated?

Choices A, C, and D are all plural verbs. Even though the blank appears after a plural noun, this noun is part of a prepositional phrase. The verb should match the singular subject *band*. The only choice with a singular verb is choice B, so B is the correct answer.

### *Conjunctions*

**Conjunctions** join words, phrases, or clauses and they show the connection between the joined pieces. **Coordinating conjunctions** connect equal parts of sentences. Coordinating conjunctions can also be used to create compound subjects and compound predicates, in addition to compound sentences.

### Coordinating Conjunctions

The **coordinating conjunctions** include: *and, but, yet, or, nor, for,* and *so*

Compound Subjects:

compound subject
Terry *and* Marissa went to the movies last Saturday.

compund subject
Either pumpkin pie *or* apple pie would be a good dessert to bring to Thanksgiving dinner.

compound subject
Neither the clownfish *nor* the goldfish liked the new fish food very much.

Compound Predicates:

compound predicate
Veronica left school *and* picked up her sister from soccer practice.

compound predicate
The cat did not take a nap *or* play with the dog yesterday.

Compound Sentences:

The rock was small, *but* it was heavy.

She drove in the night, *and* he drove in the day.

Bill dressed nicely today, *for* he must give an important presentation this afternoon.

### Correlative Conjunctions

Some examples of **correlative conjunctions** are: *either...or* | *neither...nor* | *not only...but also*. When one correlative conjunction is used, its matching correlative conjunction will be used later in the sentence.

Examples:

*Either* you are coming *or* you are staying.

He *not only* ran three miles *but also* swam 200 yards.

**Review Video: Coordinating and Correlative Conjunctions**
Visit mometrix.com/academy and enter code: 390329

### Subordinating Conjunctions

Subordinating conjunctions link dependent clauses, clauses with either a subject or a predicate, to independent clauses, clauses with both a subject and a predicate, to form a complex sentence. The subordinating conjunction will always be at the beginning of the dependent clause. When the dependent clause is at the beginning of the sentence, it will end with a comma. When the independent clause is at the beginning of the sentence, no comma is needed.

Common **subordinating conjunctions** include:

| | | |
|---|---|---|
| after | since | whenever |
| although | so that | where |
| because | unless | wherever |
| before | until | whether |
| in order that | when | while |

Examples:

I am hungry *because* I did not eat breakfast.

He went home *when* everyone left.

*While* her brother ate dinner, she played his favorite video game.

**Review Video: Subordinating Conjunctions**
Visit mometrix.com/academy and enter code: 958913

### EXAMPLE

**Which of the following is a complex sentence?**

a. Joseph went grocery shopping and put all of the groceries away at home.
b. Joseph went grocery shopping, and he put all of the groceries away at home.
c. Joseph went grocery shopping and put all of the groceries away when he got home.
d. Joseph went grocery shopping; he put all of the groceries away at home.

Choice A contains one subject and a compound predicate. Because there is only one subject, Joseph, there is only one clause. Since the sentence is made of one independent clause and a prepositional phrase, it is a simple sentence, and choice A is incorrect.

Choice B contains two clauses. The clauses are separated by a comma and a coordinating conjunction, and both are independent clauses. This sentence contains a prepositional phrase and two independent clauses, so it is a compound sentence. Choice B is incorrect.

Choice C contains two clauses. There are two subjects in the sentence, *Joseph* and *he*. Even though one clause is much shorter than the other, these subjects each go with a different clause. The first clause is independent. The second clause is dependent, as it begins with the word *when*. Since the sentence is made of one independent clause and one dependent clause, it is a complex sentence. Choice C is correct.

Choice D contains two clauses. They are both independent clauses, because they both contain a subject and a predicate, and they both form complete thoughts. Since there is no coordinating conjunction, they are linked by a semicolon. Since the sentence is made from two independent clauses, it is a compound sentence. Choice D is incorrect.

### *EXAMPLE*

**Identify the sentence that contains correlative conjunctions.**

a. She can wait for her friend's letter to arrive, or she can call her now.
b. He must leave now, or he will end up in heavy traffic when he gets on the highway.
c. When your grandfather gets here, you can greet him with a handshake or a hug.
d. I can't decide whether to go to my brother's concert or to study for my test tomorrow.

Read the answer choices carefully. Remember that correlative conjunctions appear in pairs, so there will be at least two conjunctions in the sentence. Additionally, these conjunctions will go together. The information given immediately after the first conjunction will make little sense without the information that comes after the second conjunction.

Choice A contains the conjunction *or*. Though *or* can be a correlative conjunction, in this sentence, it is used by itself to connect two independent clauses. This means it is a coordinating conjunction. There are no correlative conjunctions in this sentence, so choice A is incorrect.

Choice B contains the conjunctions *or* and *when*. Again, *or* can be a correlative conjunction. However, the sentence could end after *traffic*. The information beginning with *when* is not needed to complete the thought, and *or* and *when* do not form a pair of correlative conjunctions. Choice B is incorrect.

Choice C contains the conjunctions *when* and *or*. *When* is used to begin a dependent clause. *Or* is used to form a compound object by linking *handshake* and *hug*. These conjunctions do not work together in this sentence, so they are not correlative conjunctions. Choice C is incorrect.

Choice D contains the conjunctions *whether* and *or*. *Whether* is used to introduce one choice the speaker can make, and *or* is used to introduce an alternative choice. If the sentence ended before *or*, it would be an incomplete thought. The conjunctions *whether* and *or* go together in this sentence, and they are correlative conjunctions. Choice D is correct.

## End Punctuation

### Periods

Use a period to end all sentences except direct questions and exclamations. Periods are also used for abbreviations.

> Examples: 3 p.m. | 2 a.m. | Mr. Jones | Mrs. Stevens | Dr. Smith | Bill, Jr. | Pennsylvania Ave.

Note: An abbreviation is a shortened form of a word or phrase.

### Question Marks

Question marks should be used following a **direct question**. A polite request can be followed by a period instead of a question mark.

> **Direct Question**: What is for lunch today? | How are you? | Why is that the answer?
>
> **Polite Requests**: Can you please send me the item tomorrow. | Will you please walk with me on the track.

**Review Video: Question Marks**
Visit mometrix.com/academy and enter code: 118471

### Exclamation Marks

Exclamation marks are used after a word group or sentence that shows much feeling or has special importance. Exclamation marks should not be overused. They are saved for proper **exclamatory interjections**.

Example: We're going to the finals! | You have a beautiful car! | "That's crazy!" she yelled.

**Review Video: Exclamation Points**
Visit mometrix.com/academy and enter code: 199367

### Commas

The comma is a punctuation mark that can help you understand connections in a sentence. Not every sentence needs a comma. However, if a sentence needs a comma, you need to put it in the right place. A comma in the wrong place or a missing comma will make a sentence's meaning unclear. These are some of the rules for commas:

| Use Case | Example |
|---|---|
| Before a **coordinating conjunction** joining independent clauses in compound sentences | Bob caught three fish, and I caught two fish. |
| Between **items in a series** | I will bring the turkey, the pie, and the coffee. |
| After a **dependent clause** that **begins a complex sentence** | Before she left, Ashley turned off all of the lights in her house. |
| After **transition words** | Consequently, Joel's mother grounded him. |
| After an **introductory phrase** | After the final out, we went to a restaurant to celebrate. |

**Review Video: When To Use a Comma**
Visit mometrix.com/academy and enter code: 786797

#### Example

**Which of the following sentences is NOT missing a comma?**

a. During a play you should be quiet and respect the performers.
b. I finally fell asleep after my father turned the television off.
c. Until she finishes her vegetables she must stay at the table.
d. At the third stop sign take a right.

Remember that there are several reasons a comma may be needed in a sentence. After an introductory phrase, a transition, or a dependent clause at the beginning of a sentence are some of the most common places that a comma is needed.

Choice A is a simple sentence that begins with a prepositional phrase. Is a comma needed? Prepositional phrases can be introductory phrases, so a comma should follow them when they appear at the beginning of a sentence. The prepositional phrase in this sentence, *during a play*, functions as an introductory phrase and should be followed by a comma. Choice A is incorrect.

Choice B is a complex sentence. Are commas needed in complex sentences? When the dependent clause comes first, a comma should be used at the end of that clause. In choice B, the first clause is independent and the second is dependent. This means that no comma is needed, so the sentence is not missing any punctuation marks. Choice B is correct.

Choice C is a complex sentence. The sentence begins with *until*, which is a subordinating conjunction. This shows that the sentence begins with a dependent clause. This is a complex sentence, so the dependent clause should be followed by a comma. A comma is missing after *vegetables*, so choice C is incorrect.

Choice D is a simple sentence. Like choice A, this sentence begins with a prepositional phrase. *At the third stop sign* functions as an introductory phrase, so it should be followed by a comma. Choice D is incorrect.

EXAMPLE

**Where should a comma be added in the following sentence?**

Though the mountain is very steep he is not afraid to scale it.

a. After *Though*
b. After *mountain*
c. After *steep*
d. After *afraid*

Choice A says there should be a comma after *though*. In this sentence, *though* is a subordinating conjunction that begins a dependent clause. Remember that a comma goes at the end of a dependent clause that appears at the beginning of a sentence. *Though* is at the beginning of the clause, and there is no other need for a comma right after it. Choice A is incorrect.

Choice B says there should be a comma after *mountain*. *Mountain* is the subject of the dependent clause in this sentence. The comma should go at the end of the dependent clause. *Mountain* appears in the middle of the dependent clause, not at the end of it. Choice B is incorrect.

Choice C says there should be a comma after *steep*. *Steep* is the last word in the dependent clause that begins the sentence. Adding a comma here would correctly separate the dependent clause from the following independent clause. This is the correct place for the comma, so choice C is correct.

Choice D says there should be a comma after *afraid*. *Afraid* is the verb in the independent clause, and there is no need to separate it from the rest of the sentence. Choice D is incorrect.

*EXAMPLE*

**Where should a comma be added in the following sentence?**

However she forgot to turn the water off before she walked away from the sink.

a. After *However*
b. After *forgot*
c. After *off*
d. After *away*

Choice A says there should be a comma after *however*. *However* is a transition word that appears at the beginning of the sentence. Transitions are separated from the rest of the sentence by commas, so adding a comma after *however* is correct. Choice A is the correct answer.

Choice B says there should be a comma after *forgot*. In this sentence, *forgot* is in the middle of an independent clause. There is no reason for a comma after *forgot*, so choice B is incorrect.

Choice C says there should be a comma after *off*. This is a complex sentence, meaning it contains an independent clause and a dependent clause. While *off* is the last word in the independent clause, remember that a comma is not needed to separate clauses in a complex sentence unless the dependent clause comes first. Since the independent clause is first in this sentence, no comma is needed after *off*. Choice C is incorrect.

Choice D says there should be a comma after *away*. *Away* appears in the middle of a dependent clause, so its location in the sentence does not call for a comma. *Away* is not part of a list, transition, or introductory phrase, either. There is no need for a comma here, so choice D is incorrect.

## QUOTATION MARKS

Use quotation marks to close off **direct quotations** of a person's written or spoken words, which are also called **dialogue**. Do not use quotation marks around indirect quotations. An indirect quotation gives someone's message without using the person's exact words. Use **single quotation marks** to close off a quotation inside a quotation.

> **Direct Quote**: Nancy said, "I am waiting for Henry to arrive."
>
> **Indirect Quote**: Henry said that he is going to be late to the meeting.
>
> **Quote inside a Quote**: The teacher asked, "Has everyone read Martin Luther King's 'I Have a Dream' speech?"

Quotation marks should be used around the titles of **short works**: newspaper and magazine articles, poems, short stories, songs, television episodes, and radio programs. Titles of **long works** should be italicized when they are part of a typed composition or underlined when they are part of a handwritten composition.

Examples:

> "Rip Van Winkle" (short story by Washington Irving)
>
> "O Captain! My Captain!" (poem by Walt Whitman)

**Review Video: Quotation Marks**
Visit mometrix.com/academy and enter code: 884918

## APOSTROPHES

An apostrophe is used to show **possession** or the **deletion of letters in contractions**. An apostrophe is not needed with the possessive pronouns *his, hers, its, ours, theirs, whose*, and *yours*.

> **Singular Nouns**: David's car | a book's theme | my brother's board game
>
> **Plural Nouns that end with *-s***: the scissors' handle | boys' basketball
>
> **Plural Nouns that end without *-s***: Men's department | the people's adventure

**Review Video: Apostrophes**
Visit mometrix.com/academy and enter code: 213068

**Review Video: Punctuation Errors in Possessive Pronouns**
Visit mometrix.com/academy and enter code: 221438

### *Apostrophes in Contractions*

Contractions are combinations of words. Contractions involve taking two words, removing at least one letter from one of the words, putting an apostrophe in its place, and removing the space. For example, *does not* can be written as the contraction *doesn't*. The *o* is removed from *not* and is replaced with an apostrophe, which represents the removed letter, so it appears as *n't*. The space after does is then removed, turning *does not* into the contraction *doesn't*. Some more examples of contractions are listed below.

| First Word | Second Word | Contraction |
|---|---|---|
| Can | Not | Can't |
| Do | Not | Don't |
| She | Will | She'll |
| They | Will | They'll |
| He | Is | He's |
| It | Is | It's |
| They | Are | They're |
| I | Am | I'm |

Not all words can be used to form contractions, but many small, commonly used words can.

## Capitalization

One important part of using correct grammar is properly capitalizing words. Usually, only nouns will be capitalized, but there are some exceptions. The most important capitalization rule is that the first word of every sentence, no matter what part of speech it is, should be capitalized. Another exception is that the pronoun *I* should always be capitalized.

Proper nouns are always capitalized, but sometimes it can be tricky to decide whether or not a noun is a proper noun. Some words that are usually common nouns may become proper nouns when used with other words or phrases. Also, when words that are not nouns are used with a noun, or when a group of words are used together as one noun, those words may also need to be capitalized.

### *Titles of Books, Stories, and Essays*

Most of the words in titles of things like books, stories, and essays should be capitalized, but some should not. The very first word in a title should always be capitalized. Any other word in a title that is a noun, pronoun, adjective, verb or adverb should be capitalized. Articles, such as *a* or *the*, should not be capitalized. Short conjunctions and prepositions are usually not capitalized.

### *Abbreviations, Initials, and Acronyms*

Abbreviations are shortened versions of other words. When an abbreviation shortens, or abbreviates, a word that should be capitalized, the abbreviation's first letter should also be capitalized. When the shortened word is a noun that is not capitalized, the abbreviation should be in lowercase. Initials are usually written using the first letter from multiple words. For example, John Fitzgerald Kennedy is commonly referred to by his initials, JFK. Acronyms also use the first letter from multiple words, but they are different from initials because they form words on their own. For example, NASA is an acronym for National Aeronautics and Space Administration. Some acronyms, like NASA, omit small words, such as *and*, *of*, and *for*. When initials and acronyms are used for proper nouns, each letter should be capitalized.

The types of words and phrases in the chart below are proper nouns and should always be capitalized:

| | Description | Example |
|---|---|---|
| Historical Periods | A range of time in history that is related to specific events or circumstances | During the Romantic Period, many authors and poets wrote about their emotions. |
| Historical Events | Names of important events that happened in history | Napoleon Bonaparte led France after the French Revolution. |
| Historical Documents | Titles of important papers or compositions that are connected to historical events | The Mayflower Compact was written to create rules and expectations for the colony in Plymouth. |
| Languages | Names of the different languages that people speak | I want to learn to speak Cantonese, Spanish, and German. |
| Races and Ethnicities | Words often used to describe a person's heritage or cultural group | Malia taught her granddaughter how to hula so she could share a tradition of her Native Hawaiian heritage with her. |
| Nationalities | Words that describe which country a person is from | My teacher who moved to Canada last year is Romanian. |
| Organizations | Titles of official groups formed by people | Fewer than half of the states in America have a team in the National Basketball Association. |

### *EXAMPLE*

**Choose the correctly capitalized organization name.**

a. National Association for People who Hate Taking Naps
b. Organization for The Most Interesting People in America
c. Club for High-School Students Who love Reading
d. Nebraskan Club for Mountain Climbers

Names of organizations follow the same capitalization rules as titles. Remember that when capitalizing titles, it is important to consider each word's part of speech. Nouns, pronouns, verbs, adjectives, and adverbs are always capitalized in titles. Consider the part of speech of every word in each answer choice.

In choice A, the capitalized words include adjectives, nouns, and verbs. These words are all correctly capitalized. *For* and *who* are in lowercase. Which parts of speech are these words? *For* is a preposition. Remember that short prepositions are not usually capitalized in titles, so leaving *for* in lowercase is acceptable. *Who* is a pronoun. Pronouns should always be capitalized in titles, so this is an error. Choice A is incorrect.

In choice B, there is an incorrectly capitalized word. An article should not be capitalized in a title unless it is the first word in the title. In this choice, *the* is capitalized in the middle of the title. This is an error, so choice B is incorrect.

In choice C, each capitalized word is correct. These words include nouns, adjectives, a pronoun, and a verb. *For* and *love* are in lowercase. Since *for* is a short preposition, it is acceptable to leave it in lowercase. However, *love* is a verb in this title. Verbs must be capitalized in titles, so this is an error. Choice C is incorrect.

In choice D, the capitalized words include adjectives and nouns. Words belonging to these parts of speech should always be capitalized in titles. The only word that is in lowercase is *for*, which may be left in lowercase because it is a short preposition. All of the words in this organization name are correctly capitalized or left in lowercase, so choice D is correct!

### EXAMPLE

**Identify the capitalization mistake in the following sentences.**

> My brother and I want to open a bakery, so we discussed what we should call it. I wanted to give it a name that would form the acronym Bake, but we couldn't think of a good name using those letters. My brother suggested Bakery Brothers and said that if we ever need to abbreviate the name, we can call it Bakery Bros. or BB.

a. All of the letters in *Bake* should be capitalized.
b. *Bakery Brothers* should be in lowercase.
c. All of the letters in *Bros.* should be capitalized.
d. The second *B* in *BB* should be lowercase.

There are three types of abbreviations in these sentences. The second sentence contains an acronym, and the third sentence contains a shortened word and an initialism. Consider the different capitalization rules for each of these to identify the error in the sentences.

Choice A says that all of the letters in *Bake* should be capitalized. Even though *bake* is a verb that usually should not be capitalized at all, it is used as an acronym in this sentence. That means that each letter should be capitalized, so choice A is correct.

Choice B says that all of the letters in *Bakery Brothers* should be in lowercase. In the sentences, *Bakery Brothers* is the full name of the bakery. Since it is the name of a place, *Bakery Brothers* is a proper noun. It is correctly capitalized, so choice B is incorrect.

Choice C says that all of the letters in *Bros.* should be capitalized. *Bros.* is a shortening of *brothers*. Remember that shortened words should follow the same capitalization rules as the original word. Since the first letter of *brothers* is capitalized in the phrase *Bakery Brothers*, *Bros.* is written correctly. Choice C is incorrect.

Choice D says that the second *B* in *BB* should be in lowercase. *BB* is an initialism that takes the first letter from each word in the name *Bakery Brothers*. Remember that all of the letters in initialisms must be capitalized, so *BB* is correctly capitalized. Choice D is incorrect.

## Word Confusion

### To, Too, and Two

*To* can be an adverb or a preposition for showing direction, purpose, and relationship. A dictionary can also be used to see the many other ways to use *to* in a sentence.

> Examples: I went to the store. | I want to go with you.

*Too* is an adverb that means *also, as well, very,* or *in excess.*

> Examples: I can walk a mile too. | You have eaten too much.

*Two* is a number.

> Example: You have two minutes left.

### There, Their, and They're

*There* can be an adjective, adverb, or pronoun. Often, *there* is used to show a place or to start a sentence.

> Examples: I went there yesterday. | There is something in his pocket.

*Their* is a pronoun that is used to show ownership.

> Examples: He is their father. | This is their fourth apology this week.

*They're* is a contraction of *they are.*

> Example: Did you know that they're in town?

### Its and It's

*Its* is a possessive pronoun that shows ownership.

> Example: The guitar is in its case.

*It's* is a contraction of *it is.*

> Example: It's an honor and a privilege to meet you.

### Affect and Effect

There are two main reasons that *affect* and *effect* are so often confused: 1) both words can be used as either a noun or a verb, and 2) unlike most homophones, their usage and meanings are closely related to each other. Here is a quick explanation of the four usage options:

**Affect (n)**: feeling, emotion, or mood that is displayed

> Example: The patient had a flat *affect.* (i.e., his face showed little or no emotion)

**Affect (v)**: to alter, to change, to influence

> Example: The sunshine *affects* the plant's growth.

**Effect (n)**: a result, a consequence

> Example: What *effect* will this weather have on our schedule?

**Effect (v)**: to bring about, to cause to be

> Example: These new rules will *effect* order in the office.

### *Example*

**Choose the correct spelling from each pair of homophones in the following passage.**

> I found a unique tree in the forest. (It's/Its) trunk is blue, and it has (two/too) many branches to count. I brought some of my friends to see it, but the tree did not seem to (affect/effect) them. While (their/they're) not fascinated by the strange tree, I am!

The first pair of homophones is *it's* and *its*. Remember that the contraction *it's* is used in place of *it is*. *Its* is a possessive pronoun that shows a thing's ownership or possession. An easy way to decide whether *it's* or *its* is correct is to see how the sentence sounds with *it is*, instead. *It is trunk is blue* does not make sense. *Its trunk is blue* means that the tree has a blue trunk, so *its* is the correct choice.

The next pair of homophones is *two* and *too*. *Two* only means the number two. *Too* can mean *also* or *in excess*. Which of these makes the most sense in this sentence? *Two many branches to count* or *too many branches to count*? The correct meaning is that there is an abundance of branches, so *too* is the correct choice for this pair.

The third pair of homophones is *affect* and *effect*. Since both of these words can be used as a noun or verb, identifying the correct part of speech is a helpful first step. The part of speech is a verb, since the correct word will show what *the tree* does to *them*. *Affect* as a verb means to change or influence. *Effect* as a verb means to lead to or cause something to happen. Replace the homophone with these synonyms. Seeing the tree cannot cause or lead the speaker's friends to exist, but it can change them or influence them. *Affect* is the correct choice for this pair.

The last pair of homophones is *their* and *they're*. *Their* is a possessive pronoun used to show that multiple people or things own something. *They're* is a contraction used in place of *they are*. Replace the homophone with *they are*. Does the sentence make sense? It does because they, the speaker's friends, are not fascinated by the tree. Saying *their not fascinated* does not make sense. *They're* is the correct choice for this pair.

## Types of Essays

### Essays

Essays usually focus on one topic, subject, or goal. There are several types of essays, including informative, persuasive, and narrative. An essay's structure and formality depend on the type of essay and its goal. While narrative essays typically do not include outside sources, other types of essays often require some research and the use of primary and secondary sources.

The basic format of an essay typically has three major parts: the introduction, the body, and the conclusion. The body is further divided into the writer's main points. Most essays will have at least three main points, but essays that go into more depth can have almost any number of main points.

An essay's introduction should answer three questions:

1. What is the **subject** of the essay?

   If an essay is about a book, the answer would include the title and author of the book, as well as any additional information needed, such as the subject or argument of the book.

2. How does the essay **discuss** the subject?

   To answer this, the writer briefly summarizes the main points and the evidence supporting them to let readers know how the essay is organized and what information they can expect to read.

3. What will the essay **prove**?

   This information is in the thesis statement, usually the opening paragraph's last sentence, which clearly states the writer's message.

The body elaborates on all the main points related to the thesis, introducing one main point at a time, and includes supporting evidence with each main point. Each body paragraph should state the point in a topic sentence, which is usually the first sentence in the paragraph. The paragraph should then explain the point's meaning, support it with quotations or other evidence, and then explain how this point and the evidence are related to the thesis. The writer should then repeat this procedure in a new paragraph for each additional main point.

The conclusion restates the content of the introduction, including the thesis, to remind the reader of the essay's main argument or subject. The essay writer may also summarize the highlights of the argument or description contained in the body of the essay, following the same organization originally used in the body. For example, a conclusion might look like: Point 1 + Point 2 + Point 3 = Thesis, or Point 1 → Point 2 → Point 3 → Thesis Proof. Good organization makes essays easier for writers to compose and provides a guide for readers to follow. Well-organized essays hold attention better and are more likely to get readers to believe or agree with the writer.

### *Using Sources in Essays*

Sometimes writers use information from others in their work. This is most common in expository and persuasive writing. For an expository essay, a writer may not know all of the information that he or she needs to finish the composition. The writer may use other people's work to find the missing information and complete the composition. Persuasive writers may do research to find facts or statements from others that support their own beliefs and make their writing more persuasive. In both cases, research helps the writer find information that **supports** his or her **original work**.

Outside information must be relevant, true, and helpful to be appropriate for a composition. Writers must also be careful not to use too much outside information, since this can make the composition unoriginal. If a writer does use outside information, it is extremely important that the writer mention in the composition where the information came from. If the writer forgets or chooses not to say where the information came from, he or she has stolen someone else's work and presented it as their own. Doing this is called **plagiarism**.

## Informational Texts

Informational texts, also called instructional or expository texts, are compositions written to inform the reader about a specific topic. An informational essay can inform readers in a variety of ways, such as giving them instructions, telling them facts about the topic, or teaching them why something happens. Informational texts should be logical, meaning that they should present information in an order that the reader can easily understand, and they should include the right amount of information so the writer successfully informs his or her audience of new information.

Informational texts should also focus on a **central idea**. In the introduction of an informational text, there may be a sentence or two that clearly state the essay's central idea. This sentence, or sentences, is called a **thesis statement**. The central idea should be clear throughout the composition. By emphasizing the central idea in the introduction, body, and conclusion, the writer can ensure that the central idea is clear. One way to make sure that the central idea is emphasized is to think about the purpose of each part of the essay. The introduction prepares the reader by telling them what the rest of the essay is about, so the central idea should be **introduced** in this section. The body tells the reader the information the writer wants to tell the audience, so this **explains** the central idea and facts about it to the reader. The conclusion is used to **remind** the reader of how the information in the body is related and **restates** the central idea one final time.

### *STRUCTURES OR ORGANIZATIONAL PATTERNS IN INFORMATIONAL TEXTS*

Informational text can be **descriptive**, meaning that it gives information that can be experienced through the five senses, or it answers the questions what, who, when, where, and why. One common method of organizing informational text is to put it in a certain sequence, or order. **Chronological** texts include events in the order that they occurred, from start to finish. **How-to**, or **instructional**, texts organize information into a series of instructions in the order in which the steps should be followed. **Comparison-contrast** structures of informational text describe different ideas to their readers by pointing out how things or ideas are similar and how they are different. **Cause and effect** structures of informational text describe events that occurred and the causes or reasons for those events. **Problem and solution** structures of informational texts introduce and describe problems and offer one or more solutions for each problem described.

## ARGUMENTATIVE WRITING

In argumentative writing, the writer expresses a belief or opinion that he or she wants to lead readers to agree with. When writing an argumentative composition, the writer should first identify the **topic** his or her opinion is about. The topic may be serious or fun, as long as there is one clear topic in the composition. The next step is for the writer to determine his or her opinion on the topic and determine why he or she holds that opinion. In order to persuade others to agree with their opinion, the writer must be able to give readers reasons to support the opinion. If the writer does not know why he or she has an opinion, it will be difficult to convince readers to agree. In addition to having reasons that support their opinion, writers should prepare examples that support each of these reasons in order to strengthen their composition.

Once the writer has determined his or her topic, opinion, and reasons for having the opinion, he or she is ready to begin writing an argumentative essay. In the introduction, the writer should capture the reader's interest, introduce the topic, and reveal his or her opinion about the topic. In the body of the composition, the writer should remind the reader of the opinion and give his or her reasons for holding the opinion. If the writer has any examples, facts, or other information that supports his or her opinion or reasons for believing it, these should also be included in the body. Writers may also use a body paragraph to mention opposing opinions or beliefs and explain why they disagree with them. As in other compositions, the conclusion should remind the reader of the essay's topic and purpose, as well as remind the reader how the opinion has been explained and supported. The conclusion should also invite the reader to continue thinking about the topic and writer's opinion.

This can be done through questions or statements that lead readers to consider whether or not they agree with the author's opinion or what their own opinions are.

**Review Video: Argumentative Writing**
Visit mometrix.com/academy and enter code: 561544

### *Informative vs. Persuasive Writing*

**Informative** writing, also called explanatory or expository writing, is written to show that something is true or factual, while **persuasive** writing is written to lead the reader to agree with something that may or may not be true or factual. While persuasive text is written to **persuade** readers to agree with the author's position, informative text simply **provides information** to readers. Informative writing **informs** readers about why or how something is as it is. This can include offering new information, explaining how a process works, or describing a concept for readers.

**Review Video: Informational Text**
Visit mometrix.com/academy and enter code: 924964

### *Facts and Opinions*

Writers and readers must always be aware of the difference between fact and opinion. A **fact** can be tested and proven to be true. An **opinion**, on the other hand, is someone's personal thoughts or feelings. Opinions are often not changed by information. If an author writes that a newborn elephant is about five times taller than a newborn giraffe, then he or she is stating a fact. If the author writes that giraffes are more interesting than elephants, then he or she is giving an opinion because this cannot be proven to be true or false. Opinions are often supported by facts. For instance, the author might use a comparison between the way that giraffes eat and the way elephants eat as evidence of how giraffes are more interesting. An opinion supported by facts tends to be more convincing. On the other hand, when authors support their opinions with other opinions, readers should seriously think about and read the argument carefully to see whether it is logical and trustworthy.

**Review Video: Distinguishing Fact and Opinion**
Visit mometrix.com/academy and enter code: 870899

## Narrative Writing

Put simply, **narrative** writing tells a story. Narratives should tell stories in such a way that the readers learn something or gain understanding about a related topic or idea. Personal narratives are narratives writers create about personal experiences that were meaningful to them. Narratives should start with the story's actions or events, rather than long descriptions or introductions. However, the narrative should still include descriptions at points where they will entertain the reader or help the reader visualize or better understand the scene. To write an effective description, writers should include sensory details, asking themselves what they saw, heard, felt or touched, smelled, and tasted during the experiences they describe. In narrative writing, the details should be **concrete** rather than **abstract**. Concrete details are those that can be experienced through one of the five senses, while abstract details are not able to be experienced in this way. Using concrete details enables readers to imagine everything that the writer describes. Writers should make sure that there is a point to each story by describing what they learned from the experience they narrate.

### *Personal Narratives*

A **personal narrative** is a story about something that happened to the writer. **Personal narrative essays** are structured the same as other types of essays, as they have an introduction, body paragraphs, and a conclusion. Like other essays, the introduction of a personal narrative should contain a hook, or an opening sentence that interests the reader and prompts them to read the rest of the narrative. The introduction may also provide context for the story told in the personal narrative. One significant difference between personal narratives and other essays is that the body paragraphs of a personal narrative should contain sensory details, or imagery. A good personal narrative will give the reader a clear picture of the events and engage their emotions, and sensory details are effective at achieving these goals. The body should describe the events in chronological order, and the story should be completed in the last body paragraph. The conclusion will summarize the main idea of the personal narrative and may include information such as the writer's brief reflection on the events, how the events taught or changed the writer, or any relevant events that have happened since the events in the narrative.

### *Sensory Details*

Writers need to use vivid descriptions when writing descriptive essays. Narratives should also include descriptions of characters, things, and events. Writers should remember to describe not only the visual detail of what someone or something looks like, but details from other senses, as well. For example, they can contrast the feeling of a sea breeze to the feeling of a mountain breeze, describe how they think something inedible would taste, and compare sounds they hear in the same location at different times of day and night. Readers have trouble visualizing images or imagining sensory impressions and feelings from abstract descriptions, so concrete descriptions make these more real.

## Informational Text Example

Below is a prompt for an informational text. There is also an example of an essay that addresses the prompt. There are multiple drafts of this essay to show what kinds of changes a writer may make during the writing process to improve his or her work.

### Prompt:

One of the things that makes each person unique is the hobbies they enjoy doing in their free time. Write about a hobby you enjoy. Be sure to include information about how you became interested in the hobby.

## Rough Draft

Prepare to see your boredom disappear before your very eyes! Presto! That is what my favorite hobby did for me. Learning and performing magic tricks for my friends and family is my favorite hobby.

Every time we go to my grandparents' house, he does a card trick when we get there. Last year on my birthday, he gave me a cool deck of cards and showed me how to do a trick. I practiced it a couple of times and then tried it with some of my friends. I did it correctly with most of them, and they were so impressed! I was looking up new card tricks online when I discovered that there are other kinds of magic tricks, too. I decided to learn one to show my grandpa the next time he visited. I ended up learning five tricks that day! Since then, learning magic tricks has been my hobby.

Before I started learning magic tricks, my hobby was collecting rocks. I started collecting rocks around my neighborhood, but then I also started collecting them on vacations. I enjoyed that hobby until school started again. Then I had fewer opportunities to find cool rocks. I enjoy learning magic tricks much more, and it is something I can do any day after school. I also like learning magic tricks more that collecting things because it is more exciting. Looking at the rocks I had collected got old, but I never get tired of magic tricks!

One of my favorite things about my hobby is that I can perform magic shows. Once I have learned several new magic tricks, I get to do a magic show for my parents and my sister. If there was ever a talent show at school, I would do magic tricks as my talent. It is fun to show off the tricks I have learned, but my favorite part of doing magic shows is seeing that others enjoy my magic tricks. I love that I can share my hobby with others!

I am very thankful to my grandpa for inspiring my hobby! I believe I will always love doing magic tricks and hope I can become a better magician if I keep learning and practicing!

### Revised Draft

Prepare to see your boredom disappear before your very eyes! Presto! That is what my favorite hobby did for me. Learning and performing magic tricks for my friends and family is my favorite hobby.

Every time we go to my grandparents' house, he does a card trick when we get there. Last year on my birthday, he gave me a cool deck of cards and showed me how to do a trick. I practiced it a couple of times and then tried it with some of my friends. I did it correctly with most of them, and they were so impressed! I was looking up new card tricks online when I discovered that there are other kinds of magic tricks, too. I decided to learn one to show my grandpa the next time he visited. I ended up learning five tricks that day! Since then, learning magic tricks has been my hobby.

~~Before I started learning magic tricks, my hobby was collecting rocks. I started collecting rocks around my neighborhood, but then I also started collecting them on vacations. I enjoyed that hobby until school started again. Then I had fewer opportunities to find cool rocks. I enjoy learning magic tricks much more, and it is something I can do any day after school. I also like learning magic tricks more that collecting things because it is more exciting. Looking at the rocks I had collected got old, but I never get tired of magic tricks!~~

One of my favorite things about my hobby is that I can perform magic shows. Once I have learned several new magic tricks, I get to do a magic show for my parents and my sister. If there was ever a talent show at school, I would do magic tricks as my talent. It is fun to show off the tricks I have learned, but my favorite part of doing magic shows is seeing that others enjoy my magic tricks. I love that I can share my hobby with others!

<u>I still enjoy watching others do magic tricks, but I enjoy learning and performing them even more.</u> I am very thankful to my grandpa for inspiring my hobby! I believe I will always love doing magic tricks and hope I can become a better magician if I keep learning and practicing!

### *Revised Draft Notes*

Remember the purpose of the revising stage of the writing process. When revising, it is important to look at the whole composition. Do all of the paragraphs strengthen the composition? Do the introduction and conclusion help the reader understand the central idea and main points?

First, look at the underlined words. These are words that have been added. In the conclusion, a sentence has been added. This sentence strengthens the composition because it creates a transition from the body to the conclusion. It also gives the writer's thoughts about the details he or she included in the essay. Before, the conclusion began abruptly and only mentioned one of the writer's points from the body of the composition. After this sentence was added, the conclusion became about each of the writer's points from the body paragraphs. This sentence reminds the reader of the writer's points and the composition's central idea, instead of focusing on only one of the writer's points.

Next, look at what has been crossed out in this essay. These are words that have been removed. A whole paragraph has been omitted! Why is that? There were no huge errors, and the writing made sense. The paragraph talks about why learning magic tricks is better than the writer's former hobby. While this is related to the central idea, this information is not entirely relevant and does not offer much new information about magic tricks. This paragraph does not strengthen the composition or help the reader understand the central idea. The writer made a wise choice to remove this information and should later replace it with a paragraph that gives the reader new information about the writer's hobby, why the writer enjoys it, or something the writer has experienced through it.

## Edited Draft

Prepare to see your boredom disappear before your very eyes! Presto! ~~That is what my favorite hobby did for me.~~ Learning and performing magic tricks for my friends and family is my favorite hobby.

My interest in magic tricks was inspired by my grandpa. Every time we go to my grandparents' house, he does a card trick when we get there. Last year on my birthday, he gave me a cool deck of cards and showed me how to do a trick. I practiced it a couple of times and then tried it with some of my friends. I did it correctly with most of them, and they were so impressed! I was looking up new card tricks online when I discovered that there are other kinds of magic tricks, too. I decided to learn one to show my grandpa the next time he visited. I ended up learning five tricks that day! Since then, learning magic tricks has been my hobby.

~~Before I started learning magic tricks, my hobby was collecting rocks. I started collecting rocks around my neighborhood, but then I also started collecting them on vacations. I enjoyed that hobby until school started again. Then I had fewer opportunities to find cool rocks. I enjoy learning magic tricks much more, and it is something I can do any day after school. I also like learning magic tricks more that collecting things because it is more exciting. Looking at the rocks I had collected got old, but I never get tired of magic tricks!~~

One of my favorite things about my hobby is that I can perform magic shows. Once I have learned several new magic tricks, I get to do a magic show for my parents and my sister. ~~If there was ever a talent show at school, I would do magic tricks as my talent.~~ My sister wants me to do a magic show at her birthday party. I am so excited to do my magic tricks for a new audience! It is fun to show off the tricks I have learned, but my favorite part of doing magic shows is seeing that others enjoy my magic tricks. I love that I can share my hobby with others!

I still enjoy watching others do magic tricks, but I enjoy learning and performing them even more. I am very thankful to my grandpa for inspiring my hobby! I believe I will always love doing magic tricks and hope I can become a better magician if I keep learning and practicing!

### *EDITED DRAFT NOTES*

Since the writer has revised his or her work, the next step is to edit the composition. Remember that editing is very similar to revising, but editing usually includes paying attention to each paragraph, instead of the whole composition. Look at the changes that were made to each paragraph.

In the introduction, a sentence was removed. Why was it removed? While it said something about hobbies, it did not strengthen the composition. This sentence connects the hook to the prompt, but it does not introduce the topic or give the reader useful information. This sentence is not about the specific hobby being discussed in the composition. While it gives a transition from the hook to the thesis, a different sentence would better prepare the reader for the information in the rest of the essay.

Only one change has been made in the second paragraph. A transition has been added to the beginning of the first sentence. This helps connect this paragraph to the rest of the composition and prepares the reader for the information in the paragraph. Before, this paragraph simply described an event and explained how it led the writer to begin his or her hobby. However, the reader is not told why the paragraph is relevant until later in the paragraph. Now, the reader is told the purpose at the beginning of the paragraph. This strengthens the composition by improving how this paragraph flows with the rest of the essay.

What has been changed in the fourth paragraph? Another sentence has been crossed out, and two new ones have been added. Why? This paragraph tells why the writer enjoys doing magic shows, and it includes the example of magic shows the writer has performed for his or her family. The end of the paragraph tells the reasons why the writer has enjoyed doing the magic shows. The crossed-out sentence tells the reader that the author would do a magic act for a school talent show. This detail is relevant to the rest of the paragraph, but it does not support the paragraph's main point. The underlined sentences include supporting details that explain that the writer has an opportunity to do a show for a new audience. This example is better because it elaborates on the first example and connects the examples to the reason the writer enjoys doing magic shows. These sentences help the paragraph flow better and support the other ideas in the paragraph.

The remaining marks are left to remind the writer that the third paragraph still needs to be replaced. This information will be added before the final draft is finished.

## Final Draft

Prepare to see your boredom disappear before your very eyes! Presto! That is what happened to me when I began learning how to do magic tricks. Now, learning and performing magic tricks for my friends and family is my favorite hobby.

My interest in magic tricks was inspired by my grandpa. Every time we go to my grandparents' house, he does a card trick when we get there. Last year on my birthday, he gave me a cool deck of cards and showed me how to do a trick. I practiced it a couple of times and then tried it with some of my friends. I did it correctly with most of them, and they were so impressed! I was looking up new card tricks online when I discovered that there are other kinds of magic tricks, too. I decided to learn one to show my grandpa the next time he visited. I ended up learning five tricks that day! Since then, magic tricks have been my hobby.

While doing magic tricks is very fun, it takes practice at first. Some tricks are difficult to get the hang of because you have to do some steps very carefully. For example, for some tricks, you have to hide a small object in your hand or behind your hand. If the object is not completely hidden or if you make it too obvious that you are hiding something, the trick does not work as well. These tricks are very difficult for me to learn, so I have to practice them more than other tricks. Sometimes it takes patience, but mastering a trick is so fun that practicing is worth it!

One of my favorite things about my hobby is that I can perform magic shows. Once I have learned several new magic tricks, I get to do a magic show for my parents and my sister. My sister wants me to do a magic show at her birthday party. I am so excited to do my magic tricks for a new audience! It is fun to show off the tricks I have learned, but my favorite part of doing magic shows is seeing that others enjoy my magic tricks. I love that I can share my hobby with others!

I still enjoy watching others do magic tricks, but I enjoy learning and performing them even more. I am very thankful to my grandpa for inspiring my hobby! I believe I will always love doing magic tricks and hope I can become a better magician if I keep learning and practicing!

### *Final Draft Notes*

This is the final draft! In this draft, information has been added to the introduction, and there is a new paragraph. Now, the introduction includes a sentence that introduces the central idea of the composition and prepares the reader for the information in the rest of the essay. The new paragraph also gives new information about doing magic tricks. This paragraph describes a lesson the writer learned through doing magic tricks and gives the reader more information about the writer's experience practicing the hobby. These additions strengthen the composition by replacing weaker information with details that are more informative and engaging for the reader.

#### Evaluation

The essay answers the prompt and is on topic throughout the composition. The central idea is clear and is stated in the introduction, supported in the body, and restated in the conclusion. The thesis statement restates parts of the prompt and gives the reader a preview of the rest of the essay. The body uses well-structured paragraphs to explain the supporting details and examples and connects them to the central idea. The conclusion also emphasizes the central idea and supporting details and invites the reader to consider what they have read.

The essay is also interesting and written with a variety of sentence types. It uses transitions and good paragraph structure to make the essay easy for the reader to understand. The introduction also uses a hook to get the reader's attention and help him or her relate to the information in the essay. Not only does this essay answer the prompt and have appropriate structure, but it also makes use of good, engaging, and interesting details.

# Practice Test #1

*Questions 1 – 7 pertain to the following passage:*

**Masters of the Seas**

(1) Pirates have been sailing the seas for thousands of years. (2) The first recorded pirate raids occurred in 735 B.C. (3) During the middle ages, pirates lived mostly in Europe. (4) Later, pirates moved into the Caribbean, the South China Sea, and any other place with ships.

(5) Sometimes noblemen became pirates. (6) Some pirates were escaped slaves or criminals hiding from the law, others were gamblers, rebels, or people seeking adventure. (7) Even a few women were pirates!

(8) In spite of their different backgrounds; all pirates were looking for treasure. (9) They looked for real treasure such as gold, silver, and jewels. (10) They also looked for trading items such as spices, cloth, and tobacco. (11) In addition, pirates looked for useful items like tools, maps, and food.

(12) While many people think of pirates as part of history, there were still pirates on the seas today. (13) Modern pirates sail mostly near the coast of Africa, and they attack tanker ships and merchant ships. (14) Instead of treasure, today pirates ask for ransom money. (15) As long as there are ships sailing. (16) Pirates always will be around.

**1. In sentence 3, what change, if any, should be made to the capitalization?**

a. No change is necessary
b. Change middle ages to Middle ages
c. Change middle ages to Middle Ages
d. Change middle ages to middle Ages

**2. Which sentence is the best choice for the first sentence of paragraph 2?**

a. Sometimes noblemen became pirates
b. Although they all raided ships, pirates came from many different backgrounds
c. There were many ships on the seas, especially in the 1700s and 1800s
d. Pirates were very knowledgeable in geography, and they were all excellent sailors

**3. What revision, if any, is needed in sentence 6?**

a. No revision is necessary
b. Remove the comma between law and others
c. Change the comma between law and others to a semicolon followed by the word and
d. Change the comma between law and others to a period

**4. Which change, if any, is needed in sentence 7?**

a. No change is necessary
b. Change were to was
c. Change women to woman
d. Change few to several

**5. Which of the following choices is the most correct version of sentence 8?**

a. In spite of their different backgrounds; all pirates were looking for treasure
b. In spite of their different backgrounds, all pirates were looking for treasure
c. In spite of their different backgrounds. All pirates were looking for treasure
d. In spite of their different backgrounds; and all pirates were looking for treasure

**6. Which change, if any, works best in sentence 12?**

a. No change is necessary
b. Change were to was
c. Change were to are
d. Change were to is

**7. Which revision, if any, is needed in sentences 15 and 16?**

a. No revision is necessary
b. As long as there are ships sailing; pirates always will be around
c. As long as there are ships sailing. I think pirates always will be around
d. As long as there are ships sailing, pirates always will be around

*Alicia wrote this report all about volcanoes. She would like your help revising her report. Read the report and look for places where Alicia could make revisions or improvements. When you are finished reading, answer the questions that follow.*

*Questions 8 – 14 pertain to the following passage:*

**The Power of Volcanoes**

(1) The word *volcano* comes from *Vulcan*, the name of the ancient Roman god of fire. (2) A volcano occurs when hot, melted rock called magma breaks through the earth's crust. (3) I once saw a volcano erupt when I was on vacation in Hawaii. (4) When magma comes out on the surface of the earth and it is called lava. (5) Hot lava and ash often explode out of volcanoes, sometimes causing a lot of destruction.

(6) There are four basic types of volcanoes. (7) Shield volcanoes have broad, gentle slopes. (8) Cindercone volcanoes are pointed, kind of like pyramids. (9) Strato-volcanoes have many lairs of rock formed by hardened lava and ash from previous eruptions. (10) Dome volcanoes were shaped like steep mounds and are the result of slow-flowing lava.

(11) Whatever the type, volcanoes happen in places where the plates of the earth's crust touch each other. (12) There are many active volcanoes all over the world. (13) Some is in the United States, in places like Washington, Colorado, and Hawaii. (14) Some volcanoes are even under water, far below the surface of the ocean.

(15) When volcanoes erupt, they can change many things. (16) They can add height to mountains and even form new islands. (17) In Iceland, the island of Surtsey was formed by an erupting volcano in 1963. (18) Volcanoes can also collapse mountains. (19) At Crater Lake in Oregon, where a volcano collapsed a mountain, forming the deepest lake in the United States. (20) No matter their type or effects, everyone must agree that volcanoes are very powerful.

**8. In sentence 1, what change, if any, should be made in capitalization?**

a. No change is necessary
b. Change ancient Roman god to Ancient Roman God
c. Change ancient Roman god to ancient Roman God
d. Change ancient Roman god to ancient roman god

**9. Which sentence does not belong in paragraph 1?**

a. Sentence 1
b. Sentence 4
c. Sentence 3
d. Sentence 5

**10. What revision, if any, is needed in sentence 4?**

a. No revision is needed
b. Replace and with a comma
c Insert a comma before and
d. Replace and with a semicolon

**11. Which spelling change is needed in sentence 9?**

a. Change volcanoes to volcanos
b. Change previous to pervious
c. Change eruptions to erupshuns
d. Change lairs to layers

**12. What revision, if any, is necessary in sentence 10?**

a. No revision is necessary
b. Change were to are
c. Change were to was
d. Change were to is

**13. Which of the following is the best version of sentence 13?**

a. Some is in the United States, in places like Washington, Colorado, and Hawaii
b. Some were in the United States, in places like Washington, Colorado, and Hawaii
c. Some was in the United States, in places like Washington, Colorado, and Hawaii
d. Some are in the United States, in places like Washington, Colorado, and Hawaii

**14. Which change, if any, is needed in sentence 19?**

a. No change is needed
b. Remove the comma after Oregon
c. Remove the word where
d. Replace the comma after Oregon with a semicolon

*Questions 15 – 21 pertain to the following passage:*

**Down on the Farm**

(1) On the day of the field trip, our classroom was buzzing with excitement. (2) Finally, the time came to get on the bus. (3) I watched out the window as big buildings slipped by, then houses and then fields. (4) The bus turned down a long, gravel driveway and stopped by a big red barn. (5) We were at the farm!

(6) We learned that Farmer Jones and his wife grew corn and pumpkins and raised cows and chickens. (7) First, we took a tour of the farm. (8) They had several farm workers to help take care of the farm. (9) Farmer Jones and his wife also have a small market where they sold there crops and some crops from other farmers who lived nearby.

(10) I loved walking through the cornfield with the dry stalks rustling above my head. (11) Farmer Jones also let me feed a calf from a bottle, and I loved feeling it suck and tug to get at the milk. (12) When we were done seeing the farm. (13) Farmer Jones took us all up to the market for some fresh, hot corn on the cob. (14) It was so yummy!

(15) When the time came to get back on the bus, no one wanted to leave. (16) We thanked Farmer Jones and headed back to town. (17) I loved visiting the farm and seeing how Farmer Jones lived maybe I will decide to be a farmer someday.

**15. What spelling change, if any, is needed in sentence 1?**

a. No change is needed
b. Change classroom to class room
c. Change buzzing to buzing
d. Change excitement to excitment

**16. Which of the following choices is the best version of sentence 3?**

a. I watched out the window as big buildings slipped by, then houses and then fields
b. I watched out the window as big buildings slipped by, then houses; and then fields
c. I watched out the window as big buildings slipped by, then houses, and then fields
d. I watched out the window as big buildings slipped by, then houses; then fields

**17. Which sentence is the best choice for the first sentence of paragraph 2?**

a. Sentence 6
b. Sentence 7
c. Sentence 8
d. Sentence 9

**18. Which revision, if any, is needed in sentence 9?**

a. No revision is needed
b. Change have to had
c. Change have to has
d. Change have to having

**19. Which of the following choices is the proper spelling choice for sentence 9?**

a. They're
b. There
c. Thier
d. Their

**20. What revision, if any, is needed in sentences 12 and 13?**

a. No revision is needed
b. Change the period to a semicolon
c. Add Then at the beginning of sentence 13
d. Change the period to a comma

**21. What change, if any, is necessary in sentence 17?**

a. No change is necessary
b. Insert a comma after lived
c. Insert a period after lived
d. Insert a semicolon and and after lived

*Questions 22 -28 pertain to the following passage:*

**Some People Never Learn**

(1) One lazy Sunday afternoon, all the boys in our neighborhood decide to play football in the big field on the corner. (2) There used to be a gas station there, but a construction company knocked it down. (3) My brother, Seth, went to play, so I went along to watch. (4) It had rained all morning. (5) So the field was muddy and slick. (6) On the second play of the game, a big boy crashed into Seth and knocked him to the ground.

(7) I rushed over to Seth. (8) He was pale and shaking, and he was holding his arm. (9) He told me to run home and get Mom. (10) Mom came with the car, and we help Seth get in and buckle his seatbelt. (11) Then we did drive him to the hospital.

(12) In the emergency room, the doctors and nurses began working on Seth. (13) They sent him for x-rays and gave him some pills to make the pain better. (14) Then a doctor came in and said Seth broke his upper arm. (15) Seth's arm would have to be in a sling for six weeks to help it heal.

(16) For six long weeks, I helped Mom take care of Seth he needed help with almost everything. (17) Lucky for him, he didn't have to do chores for six weeks, and he even got to skip some of his schoolwork. (18) Finally Seth's arm was better, and he could take off the sling. (19) The very next day, Seth was back out in the field playing football. (20) Some people never learn!

**22. What change, if any, is needed in sentence 1?**

a. No change is needed
b. Change decide to decides
c. Change decide to decided
d. Change decide to deciding

**23. Which sentence does not belong in this essay?**

a. Sentence 1
b. Sentence 2
c. Sentence 6
d. Sentence 9

**24. What revision, if any, is needed in sentences 4 and 5?**

a. No revision is needed
b. Replace the period with a comma
c. Replace the period with a semicolon
d. Insert and at the beginning of sentence 5

**25. Which change, if any, is needed in sentence 6?**

a. No change is needed
b. Insert a comma after Seth
c. Remove the comma after game
d. Insert a semicolon after Seth

**26. Which of the following is the most correct version of sentence 11?**

a. Then we did drive him to the hospital
b. Then we drived him to the hospital
c. Then we would drive him to the hospital
d. Then we drove him to the hospital

**27. What revision, if any, is necessary in sentence 16?**

a. No revision is necessary
b. Insert a comma after Seth
c. Remove the comma after weeks
d. Insert a period after Seth

**28. What change, if any, is needed in sentence 18?**

a. No change is needed
b. Remove the comma after better
c. Insert a comma after Finally
d. Insert a semicolon after better

## Writing Prompt

Write about the best gift you ever received.

*Sample Written Piece for Writing Prompt:*

The best gift I ever received was my puppy, Bear. It was a snowy Christmas morning, and all the presents had been opened. Then my parents brought out one more box. It was moving and whining. They gave it to me, and I opened it. It was Bear!

Ever since then, Bear has been my best friend. He sleeps in my bed with me. He loves to play with me and learn new tricks. Every day when I come home from school, Bear is waiting for me.

Bear will always be my best gift because he is always there for me. I can tell him anything. Even though he is getting bigger, he still loves me, just like he did when he was a little puppy. I am so glad Bear is mine.

# Answer Key and Explanations

**1. C:** The term *Middle Ages* refers to a specific period in history, and the name of a specific historical period always should be capitalized. Options A, B, and D all offer improper capitalization, making these choices incorrect.

**2. B:** The topic sentence of a paragraph should introduce the main idea of the paragraph. Option B begins with a transition from paragraph 1 by mentioning that all pirates raid ships. It then introduces the topic of paragraph 2, which discusses the diverse background of pirates. Option A, the current topic sentence, discusses one possible background for pirates, but it does not represent fully the main idea of the paragraph. Options C and D are similar, both discussing an aspect of pirates, but these options do not introduce the overall main idea of paragraph 2.

**3. D:** Sentence 6 is a type of run-on sentence called a comma splice. It contains two complete sentences joined only by a comma. The best option for correcting this sentence is to replace the comma with a period, creating two separate sentences. Options A and B retain the run-on structure of the sentence, making them incorrect options. Option C uses a semicolon to separate the independent clauses, but it unnecessarily adds the word *and* to the sentence, making it an incorrect option.

**4. A:** Sentence 7 is correct as it is written. Option B is incorrect because the subject of the sentence is plural, so a plural verb is necessary. Option C is incorrect because the sentence discusses more than one woman, making *women* the correct word choice. Option D is incorrect because changing *few* to *several* creates an awkward and improper sentence.

**5. B:** The first part of sentence 8 is an introductory phrase, which is dependent, so it cannot stand on its own. A comma is the most appropriate punctuation to join an introductory phrase with its associated independent clause. Options A and D are not correct because a semicolon is not an appropriate punctuation choice for joining an introductory phrase with its associated independent clause. Option C is incorrect because the introductory phrase cannot be followed by a period, since it cannot stand on its own as a sentence.

**6. C:** Sentence 12 is written in present tense and has a plural subject, so the present tense, plural verb *are* is the best choice for this sentence. Option A is incorrect because it uses a past tense verb when the sentence is written in present tense. Option B is incorrect because it uses a past tense, singular verb when the sentence is written in present tense and the subject is plural. Option D is incorrect because it uses a singular verb when the subject of the sentence is plural.

**7. D:** Sentence 15 is a sentence fragment. Careful reading shows that the best correction option connects the fragment of sentence 15 to sentence 16 with a comma, creating a single, strong sentence. Option A is incorrect because it retains sentence 15 as a fragment. Option B is incorrect because a semicolon cannot connect a dependent clause to an independent clause. Option C is incorrect because it only adds the words *I think*, retaining sentence 15 as a fragment.

**8. A:** is the best choice because the current capitalization is correct, since the only proper noun in the sentence is *Roman*. B is not the best choice because it capitalizes *Ancient* and *God*, neither of which are proper nouns in this context. C is not the best choice because it capitalizes *God*, which is not a proper noun in this context. D is not the best choice because it does not capitalize *roman*, which is a proper noun.

**9. C:** is the best choice because sentence 3 describes a personal experience that does not belong in a factual essay about volcanoes. A, B, and D are not the best choices because sentences 1, 4, and 5 all are essential to develop factual information about volcanoes.

**10. B:** is the best choice because the sentence contains a dependent introductory clause, and a dependent introductory clause always should be separated from the main clause of the sentence with a comma. A and C are not the best choices because they both create a sentence fragment. C is not the best choice because a semicolon cannot join a dependent clause to an independent clause.

**11. D:** is the best choice because *layers* is a better word choice than *lairs* in this sentence. A, B, and C are not the best choices because they all change properly spelled words to misspelled versions.

**12. B:** is the best choice because the subject of the sentence is plural and the essay is written in present tense, making *are* the right choice. A is not the best choice because *were* is a past-tense verb, and this passage is written in present tense. C is not the best choice because *was* is a singular, past-tense verb, and this sentence has a plural subject and is written in present tense. D is not the best choice because *is* is a singular verb, and the subject of this sentence is plural.

**13. D:** is the best choice because this sentence has a plural subject, and this essay is written in present tense, so *are* is right choice. A is not the best choice because *is* is a singular verb, and the subject of this sentence is plural. B is not the best choice because *were* is a past-tense verb, and this essay is written in present tense. C is not the best choice because *was* is a singular, past-tense verb, and this sentence has a plural subject and is written in present tense.

**14. C:** is the best choice because removing *where* changes the sentence from a dependent clause to a complete sentence. A, B, and D are not the best choices because they all retain the dependent clause, making the sentence a fragment—thus unable to stand on its own.

**15. A:** is the best choice because there are no misspelled words in the sentence. B, C, and D are not the best choices because they all change properly spelled words to misspelled versions.

**16. C:** is the best option because items in a series always should be separated by commas, including a comma just before the conjunction. A is not the best choice because it omits the comma before the conjunction. B and D are not the best choices because they both improperly use a semicolon to separate items in a series when those items contain no internal commas.

**17. B:** is the best choice because it clearly establishes the overall topic of the paragraph, which is what the topic sentence of a paragraph should do. A, C, and D are not the best choices because they all offer details and specifics instead of establishing a broad overview of the paragraph.

**18. B:** is the best choice because this essay is written in past tense. A and C are not the best choices because *have* and *has* are both present-tense verbs, and this essay is written in past tense. D is not the best choice because *having* is a gerund form of the verb and is inappropriate for this sentence.

**19. D:** is the best choice because *their* is the proper spelling for a plural personal pronoun showing ownership. A is not the best choice because *they're* is a contraction for *they are*, which does not fit in the sentence. B is not the best choice, because *there* refers to location, which does not fit in the sentence. C is not the best choice because it is misspelled.

**20. D:** is the best choice because sentence 12 actually is a dependent clause that should function as an introductory element to the independent clause in sentence 13, and an introductory dependent clause should be joined to the corresponding independent clause with a comma. A and C are not the best choices because they retain sentence 12 as a sentence fragment. B is not the best choice because a semicolon should not join a dependent clause to an independent clause.

**21. C:** is the best choice because adding a period eliminates the run-on sentence by creating two complete sentences. A is not the best choice because it retains the run-on sentence structure. B is not the best choice because it creates a comma splice, another type of run-on sentence. D is not the best choice because a semicolon should not be used with a conjunction to join two independent clauses.

**22. C:** is the best choice because *decided* is a past-tense verb, and this passage is written in past tense. A is not the best choice because *decide* is a present-tense verb, and this passage is written in past tense. B is not the best choice because *decides* is a singular, present-tense verb, and this sentence has a plural subject and is written in past tense. D is not the best choice because *deciding* is a gerund form of the verb, which is not appropriate in this sentence.

**23. B:** is the best choice because sentence 2 gives unnecessary details unrelated to the progression of this story. A, C, and D are not the best choices because sentences 1, 6, and 9 all offer relevant information important to the development of the story.

**24. B:** is the best choice because sentence 5 is a dependent clause that needs to be combined with sentence 4 through the use of a comma to form a complete sentence. A and D are not the best choices because they both retain sentence 5 as a sentence fragment. C is not the best choice because a semicolon should not join an independent clause to a dependent clause.

**25. A:** is the best choice because the sentence is correct as written. B is not the best choice because it inserts an unnecessary and incorrect comma. C is not the best choice because it deletes the necessary comma after the introductory phrase. D is not the best choice because it inserts an unnecessary and incorrect semicolon.

**26. D:** is the best choice because it uses the simple past-tense verb *drove*, which is appropriate for this story, since it is written in past tense. A and B are not the best choices because they both use awkward and incorrect verb forms. C is not the best choice because *would drive* is a future-tense verb, and this story is written in past tense.

**27. D:** is the best choice because it eliminates the run-on sentence and creates two complete sentences. A and C are not the best choices because they both retain the run-on sentence structure. B is not the best choice because separating two independent clauses with only a comma creates a comma splice, a type of run-on sentence.

**28. C:** is the best choice because *Finally* is an introductory word in this sentence, so it should be separated from the rest of the sentence with a comma. A is not the best choice because it does not separate the introductory word from the rest of the sentence. B is not the best choice because it removes the necessary comma separating two independent clauses joined by a coordinating conjunction. D is not the best choice because a semicolon should not be used with a coordinating conjunction to join two independent clauses.

# Practice Test #2

*Questions 1 – 7 pertain to the following passage:*

**Clara Barton: A Heart for Helping**

(1) Clara barton was born on Christmas in 1821. (2) She lived in North Oxford, Massachusetts, and was the youngest of five children. (3) Although she loved sports, reading, and horseback riding, Clara mostly enjoyed helping people. (4) In fact, when she was only 11. (5) Clara spent two years caring for her brother after he suffered a serious injury.

(6) Clara becomes a teacher while she was still a teenager because she loved to help so much. (7) After teaching for many years, Clara moved to Washington D.C. to work in the Patent Office, where she gave permits to new inventors. (8) In 1861, the Civil War began, and Clara used her free time to gather supplies for soldiers.

(9) In 1862, Clara started traveling to battlefields to help wounded soldiers and deliver food and supplies. (10) Even though she was not a nurse, Clara saved the lives of many soldiers. (11) Nurses were in great demand during the Civil War. (12) When the war ended, she continued to give speeches to people about the bad conditions on battlefields. (13) Many people heard Clara speak.

(14) In 1869, Clara traveled to Switzerland to visit some friends. (15) While there, she learned about a new organization called the International Red Cross, Clara began working with them. (16) In 1881, she returned to the United States and established the American Red Cross. (17) Then Clara spends the rest of her life doing what she loved best: helping people.

**1. Which version of sentence 1 has the most correct capitalization?**

a. Clara barton was born on Christmas in 1821
b. Clara Barton was born on Christmas in 1821
c. Clara Barton was born on christmas in 1821
d. Clara barton was born on christmas in 1821

**2. What revision, if any, is needed in sentences 4 and 5?**

a. No revision is needed
b. Remove the period
c. Replace the period with a semicolon
d. Replace the period with a comma

**3. What change, if any, is necessary in sentence 6?**

a. No change is necessary
b. Change loved to loves
c. Change becomes to became
d. Change was to were

**4. What spelling correction, if any, is needed in sentence 9?**

a. No correction is needed
b. Change traveling to travelling
c. Change battlefields to battlefeilds
d. Change soldiers to souldiers

**5. Which sentence does not belong in this essay?**

a. Sentence 4
b. Sentence 7
c. Sentence 11
d. Sentence 15

**6. What revision, if any, is needed in sentence 15?**

a. No revision is needed
b. Replace the comma after Cross with a period
c. Remove the comma after Cross
d. Replace the comma after there with a semicolon

**7. What change, if any, is necessary in sentence 17?**

a. No change is necessary
b. Replace helping with helped
c. Replace loved with loves
d. Replace spends with spent

*Questions 8 – 14 pertain to the following passages:*

**Amazing Pandas**

(1) When a baby panda is born, it is about the size of a breakfast sausage. (2) Tiny and almost furless, it snuggled close to its mother. (3) The baby panda stays very near its mother for the first two months of life. (4) Because until it is two months old, the panda's eyes cannot open. (5) It relies on its mother for everything.

(6) Even when the baby panda's eyes are open, it still needs its mother for food. (7) Baby pandas nurse from their mothers up to eight times a day until they are 18 months old. (8) During this time they also chew on bamboo but this is just for fun. (9) Their teeth are not strong enough to really eat the bamboo.

(10) Bamboo does not have many vitamins and calories, though, so pandas must spend up to 14 hours a day eating just to stay full! (11) Sometime between 12 and 18 months of age, pandas begin really eating bamboo. (12) Even so, they do not wander far from home; pandas stay with their mothers until they are full grown.

(13) When a full grown panda is about five feet long and weighs about 200 pounds. (14) They live in the forests of China, although many now live in zoos and other places. (15) In fact, there were only about 1600 pandas left in the wild because their habitats have been destroyed to build cities. (16) People need to care for pandas so these amazing animals will always be with us.

**8. What change, if any, is needed in sentence 2?**

a. No change is needed
b. Change furless to fur-less
c. Change snuggled to snuggles
d. Change its to it's

**9. What revision, if any, is necessary in sentences 3 and 4?**

a. No revision is necessary
b. Replace the period with a comma
c. Replace the period with a semicolon
d. Remove the period

**10. What change, if any, is needed in sentence 8?**

a. No change is needed
b. Insert a period after bamboo
c. Insert a comma after bamboo
d. Insert a semicolon after bamboo

**11. Which sentence is the best choice for the first sentence of paragraph 3?**

a. Sentence 10
b. Sentence 12
c. Sentence 9
d. Sentence 11

**12. What revision, if any, is necessary in sentence 12?**

a. No revision is necessary
b. Replace the semicolon with a comma
c. Remove the comma after so
d. Change the period to an exclamation point

**13. What change, if any, is needed in sentence 13?**

a. No change is needed
b. Remove the period to combine sentence 13 with sentence 14
c. Insert a comma after long
d. Remove the word When

**14. What revision, if any, is necessary in sentence 15?**

a. No revision is necessary
b. Change were to are
c. Change 1600 to sixteen hundred
d. Change their to there

*Questions 15 – 21 pertain to the following passage:*

**Niagara Falls**

(1) Last Summer, my family went on a trip to Niagara Falls in New York. (2) Niagara Falls is a famous waterfall that flows between the United States and Canada. (3) When I first saw the falls. (4) I couldn't believe it. (5) It was huge! (6) I had never seen so much water in my life.

(7) To get a better look at the falls, we decided to take a boat ride to the base of the falls, where the waterfall crashes into the river. (8) We got on a boat with a lot of other people. (9) Every person was given a blue plastic rain poncho. (10) As we got closer to the bottom of the falls, I knew why. (11) The water sprayed up like it was raining, and the crashing is so loud I couldn't even hear myself yell.

(12) We saw another boat, far below us, headed for the base of Niagara Falls. (13) When the boat ride was over, we drove back to the top of the falls and walked along the sidewalk. (14) The falls was so big it made the boat look like a toy and the people look like tiny insects.

(15) Before we left Niagara Falls, I bought some postcards at a gift shop. (16) When we got home, I used the post cards to make a new page for my scrapbook. (17) I also wrote down some of my memories from the trip. (18) Then I will always remember my trip to Niagara Falls.

**15. Which of the following versions of sentence 1 contains proper capitalization?**

a. Last Summer, my family went on a trip to Niagara Falls in New York
b. Last summer, my family went on a trip to niagara falls in New York
c. Last summer, my family went on a trip to Niagara Falls in New York
d. Last Summer, my family went on a trip to Niagara Falls in new york

**16. What revision, if any, is necessary in sentences 3 and 4?**

a. No revision is necessary
b. Replace the period with a comma
c. Remove the period
d. Replace the period with and

**17. What change, if any, is needed in sentence 11?**

a. No change is needed
b. Change sprayed to sprays
c. Change was to is
d. Change is to was

**18. Which sentence is the best choice as the first sentence of paragraph 3?**

a. Sentence 12
b. Sentence 13
c. Sentence 11
d. Sentence 14

**19. Which revision, if any, is necessary in sentence 14?**

a. No revision is necessary
b. Insert a comma after big
c. Insert a semicolon after toy
d. Insert a comma after tiny

**20. Which of the following reflects the correct spelling?**

a. Niagra Falls
b. Nyagra Falls
c. Niagara Falls
d. Niagira Falls

**21. What change, if any, is needed in sentence 18?**

a. No change is needed
b. Change remember to remembered
c. Change will to would
d. Change Then to Now

*Questions 22 – 28 pertain to the following passage:*

**A Night to Be Remembered**

(1) At the beginning of the year, my teacher announced that our school was going to have a speech contest. (2) It sounded like fun. (3) So I decided to enter. (4) I thought and thought about what to say in my speech. (5) Then I go to the library and did some research.

(6) I decided to write my speech about the life and accomplishments of Dr. Martin Luther King Jr. (7) He is one of my favorite people, and I wrote the best speech ever. (8) When I was done, I read the speech to my parents. (9) My dad once gave a speech to the city council. (10) They loved it!

(11) On the night of the speech contest, I was very nervous. (12) My stomach was flip-flopping even through I knew my speech by heart. (13) When it was my turn, I took a deep breath, stood up, and gave my speech perfectly. (14) Everyone clapped, and I sat down. (15) Then I had to wait for the judges' decision.

(16) After what seemed like forever, the head judge stood up and said it was a close concert and everyone did well. (17) Then he announced that I won first place! (18) I was so surprised that my head was spinning and my knees were wobbly. (19) After everyone cheered, and my parents took me out for ice cream. (20) It was a night I will never forget.

**22. What revision, if any, is needed in sentences 2 and 3?**

a. No revision is needed
b. Replace the period with a comma
c. Remove the period
d. Insert And at the beginning of sentence 3

**23. What change, if any, is necessary in sentence 5?**

a. No change is necessary
b. Change go to did go
c. Change go to went
d. Change did to done

**24. Which version of sentence 6 reflects correct capitalization?**

a. I decided to write my speech about the life and accomplishments of Dr. Martin Luther King Jr.
b. I decided to write my speech about the life and accomplishments of dr. Martin Luther King Jr.
c. I decided to write my speech about the life and accomplishments of Dr. Martin luther King jr.
d. I decided to write my speech about the life and accomplishments of Dr. Martin Luther King jr.

**25. Which sentence does not belong in this story?**

a. Sentence 2
b. Sentence 7
c. Sentence 9
d. Sentence 15

**26. What spelling correction, if any, is needed in sentence 12?**

a. No correction is needed
b. Change stomach to stomache
c. Change flip-flopping to flipflopping
d. Change through to though

**27. Which revision, if any, is necessary in the wording of sentence 16?**

a. No revision is necessary
b. Change head to heard
c. Change well to good
d. Change concert to contest

**28. What change, if any, is needed in sentence 19?**

a. No change is needed
b. Remove the word After
c. Remove the comma after cheered
d. Replace the comma after cheered with a semicolon

## Writing Prompt

Write about your favorite vacation.

*Sample Written Piece for Writing Prompt:*

> My favorite vacation ever was when my family went to Jamaica last summer. We rode on an airplane and landed in Jamaica in the afternoon. The weather was sunny and very hot, but our hotel was nice and cool.
>
> On our second day in Jamaica, we went to Dunn's River Falls. It is an awesome waterfall, and you can climb up to the top. We also visited a craft market where people sold necklaces and coasters and things they had carved out of wood and bamboo. Back at the hotel, some of our best times were spent swimming in the huge pool.

When the time came to leave Jamaica, I was very sad to go. I knew I would miss all the fun times I had there. I will always remember my family trip to Jamaica. It was the best vacation I ever had.

# Answer Key and Explanations

**1. B:** is the best choice because *Clara Barton* and *Christmas* both are proper nouns and should be capitalized. A is not the best choice because *Clara Barton* is a proper noun and both parts of the name should be capitalized. C is not the best choice because *Christmas* is a proper noun and should be capitalized. D is not the best choice because *Clara Barton* and *Christmas* all are proper nouns and should be capitalized.

**2. D:** is the best choice because sentence 4 actually is an introductory, dependent clause for sentence 5, and an introductory clause links to the corresponding independent clause with a comma. A is not the best choice because it retains sentence 4 as a sentence fragment. B is not the best choice because it omits the necessary comma after the introductory dependent clause. C is not the best choice because a semicolon should not link a dependent clause with an independent clause.

**3. C:** is the best choice because this passage is written in past tense and *became* is the past-tense verb form. A is not the best choice because *becomes* is a present-tense verb, and this passage is written in past tense. B is not the best choice because *loves* is a present-tense verb, and this passage is written in past tense. D is not the best choice because *were* is a plural verb, and the subject of the sentence is singular.

**4. A:** is the best choice because all words in the sentence currently are spelled correctly. B, C, and D are not the best choices because they all change properly spelled words to misspelled versions.

**5. C:** is the best choice because sentence 11 offers a fact that is irrelevant to this essay about Clara Barton. A, B, and D are not the best choices because sentences 4, 7, and 15 all are necessary for the development of this essay.

**6. B:** is the best choice because it eliminates the run-on sentence by creating two separate, complete sentences. A, C, and D are not the best choices because they all retain the run-on sentence structure.

**7. D:** is the best choice because it replaces the present-tense verb *spends* with the past-tense verb *spent*, and this passage is written in past tense. A is not the best choice because *spends* is a present-tense verb, and this passage is written in past tense. B is not the best choice because it replaces the gerund *helping* with *helped*, and the gerund form is required in this sentence. C is not the best choice because *loves* is a present-tense verb, and this passage is written in past tense.

**8. C:** is the best choice because *snuggles* is a present-tense verb and this passage is written in present tense. A is not the best choice because *snuggled* is a past-tense verb and this passage is written in present tense. B and D are not the best choices because they both replace appropriate words with wrong word forms.

**9. B:** is the best choice because sentence 4 is a dependent clause that should link to the independent clause in sentence 3 with a comma to create a complete sentence. A is not the best choice because it retains sentence 4 as a sentence fragment. C is not the best choice because a semicolon should not join an independent clause to a dependent clause. D is not the best choice because a comma is necessary when joining a dependent clause to an independent clause.

**10. C:** is the best choice because a comma should be used just before a coordinating conjunction that connects two independent clauses. A is not the best choice because it omits the necessary comma before the conjunction. B is not the best choice because a period is unnecessary in this sentence. D is not the best choice because a semicolon should not be used with a coordinating conjunction to join two independent clauses.

**11. D:** is the best choice because sentence 11 gives broad information about the topic of the paragraph, making it the best choice as the first sentence of the paragraph. A, B, and C are not the best choices because sentences 10, 12, and 9 all offer specific details about the eating habits of pandas, but they are not broad enough to serve as the topic sentence of the paragraph.

**12. A:** is the best choice because the sentence is correct as written. B is not the best choice because replacing the semicolon with a comma creates a comma splice, a type of run-on sentence. C is not the best choice because it omits a necessary comma after the introductory phrase. D is not the best choice because the sentence is a declarative statement, not an exclamation.

**13. D:** is the best choice because removing *When* allows the sentence to stand on its own as a proper sentence. A and C are not the best choices because they both retain sentence 13 as a sentence fragment. B is not the best choice because sentence 13 and sentence 14 are not closely related enough to be combined.

**14. B:** is the best choice because *are* is a present-tense verb, and this passage is written in present tense. A is not the best choice because *were* is a past-tense verb, and this passage is written in present tense. C is not the best choice because numbers over ten should be written in numeric form instead of in words. D is not the best choice because *there* is the proper form for this sentence.

**15. C:** is the best choice because summer is not a proper noun, but Niagara Falls and New York are proper nouns and require capitalization. A is not the best choice because summer is not a proper noun and should not be capitalized. B is not the best choice because Niagara Falls is a proper noun and should be capitalized. D is not the best choice because New York is a proper noun and should be capitalized.

**16. B:** is the best choice because sentence 3 is an introductory, dependent clause that needs to be joined with a comma to the independent clause in sentence 4. A is not the best choice because it retains sentence 3 as a sentence fragment. C is not the best choice because it omits the necessary comma after the introductory clause. D is not the best choice because it turns the combined sentence 3 and 4 into a long sentence fragment.

**17. D:** is the best choice because *was* is a past-tense verb, and this passage is written in past tense. A is not the best choice because *is* is a present-tense verb, and this passage is written in past tense. B and C are not the best choices because they both change appropriate past-tense verbs to inappropriate present-tense verbs.

**18. B:** is the best choice because sentence 13 introduces the broad, overall topic of the paragraph. A and D are not the best choices because sentences 12 and 14 offer details that build on the main topic of the paragraph, making them unsuited as topic sentences. C is not the best choice because sentence 11 belongs in paragraph 2 rather than in paragraph 3.

**19. A:** is the best choice because the sentence is correct as written. B is not the best choice because it breaks up the sentence with an unnecessary comma. C is not the best choice because it separates a compound subject with an unnecessary semicolon. D is not the best choice because it inserts a comma between an adjective and the noun it modifies.

**20. C:** is the best choice because it reflects the correct spelling of Niagara Falls. A, B, and D are not the best choices because they all are spelled incorrectly.

**21. D:** is the best choice because *Now* is in present tense and fits the tone and present tense of the sentence. A and C are not the best choices because they both use future-tense words, and this sentence is written in present tense. B is not the best choice because *remembered* is a past-tense verb, and this sentence is written in present tense.

**22. B:** is the best choice because sentence 3 is a dependent clause that should be joined to the independent clause in sentence 2 with a comma. A and D are not the best choices because they both retain sentence 3 as a sentence fragment. B is not the best choice because a comma is necessary to separate two clauses joined by a coordinating conjunction.

**23. C:** is the best choice because *went* is a past-tense verb, and this passage is written in past tense. A is not the best choice because *go* is a present-tense verb, and this passage is written in past tense. B and D are not the best choices because they use improper verb forms.

**24. A:** is the best choice because it contains the most appropriate capitalization. B is not the best choice, because Dr. is a title and should be capitalized. C is not the best choice because Luther is a proper noun and Jr. is a suffix, both of which should be capitalized. D is not the best choice because Jr. is a suffix and should be capitalized.

**25. C:** is the best choice because sentence 9 contains information irrelevant to the story. A, B, and D are not the best choices because sentences 2, 7, and 15 all contribute important information to the development of this story.

**26. D:** is the best choice because *though* is the most appropriate word for this sentence. A is not the best choice because *through* is not the most appropriate word for this sentence. B and C are not the best choices because they both change properly-spelled words to misspelled words.

**27. D:** is the best choice because *contest* is the best word choice for this sentence. A is not the best choice because *concert* is not the best word choice for this sentence. B and C are not the best choices because they both change appropriate word choices to inappropriate word choices.

**28. B:** is the best choice because removing the word *After* allows the sentence to stand on its own as a complete sentence. A is not the best choice because it retains sentence 19 as a sentence fragment. B and C are not the best choices because they both make unnecessary punctuation changes and retain sentence 19 as a sentence fragment.

# How to Overcome Test Anxiety

Just the thought of taking a test is enough to make most people a little nervous. A test is an important event that can have a long-term impact on your future, so it's important to take it seriously and it's natural to feel anxious about performing well. But just because anxiety is normal, that doesn't mean that it's helpful in test taking, or that you should simply accept it as part of your life. Anxiety can have a variety of effects. These effects can be mild, like making you feel slightly nervous, or severe, like blocking your ability to focus or remember even a simple detail.

If you experience test anxiety—whether severe or mild—it's important to know how to beat it. To discover this, first you need to understand what causes test anxiety.

## Causes of Test Anxiety

While we often think of anxiety as an uncontrollable emotional state, it can actually be caused by simple, practical things. One of the most common causes of test anxiety is that a person does not feel adequately prepared for their test. This feeling can be the result of many different issues such as poor study habits or lack of organization, but the most common culprit is time management. Starting to study too late, failing to organize your study time to cover all of the material, or being distracted while you study will mean that you're not well prepared for the test. This may lead to cramming the night before, which will cause you to be physically and mentally exhausted for the test. Poor time management also contributes to feelings of stress, fear, and hopelessness as you realize you are not well prepared but don't know what to do about it.

Other times, test anxiety is not related to your preparation for the test but comes from unresolved fear. This may be a past failure on a test, or poor performance on tests in general. It may come from comparing yourself to others who seem to be performing better or from the stress of living up to expectations. Anxiety may be driven by fears of the future—how failure on this test would affect your educational and career goals. These fears are often completely irrational, but they can still negatively impact your test performance.

## Elements of Test Anxiety

As mentioned earlier, test anxiety is considered to be an emotional state, but it has physical and mental components as well. Sometimes you may not even realize that you are suffering from test anxiety until you notice the physical symptoms. These can include trembling hands, rapid heartbeat, sweating, nausea, and tense muscles. Extreme anxiety may lead to fainting or vomiting. Obviously, any of these symptoms can have a negative impact on testing. It is important to recognize them as soon as they begin to occur so that you can address the problem before it damages your performance.

The mental components of test anxiety include trouble focusing and inability to remember learned information. During a test, your mind is on high alert, which can help you recall information and stay focused for an extended period of time. However, anxiety interferes with your mind's natural processes, causing you to blank out, even on the questions you know well. The strain of testing during anxiety makes it difficult to stay focused, especially on a test that may take several hours. Extreme anxiety can take a huge mental toll, making it difficult not only to recall test information but even to understand the test questions or pull your thoughts together.

## Effects of Test Anxiety

Test anxiety is like a disease—if left untreated, it will get progressively worse. Anxiety leads to poor performance, and this reinforces the feelings of fear and failure, which in turn lead to poor performances on subsequent tests. It can grow from a mild nervousness to a crippling condition. If allowed to progress, test anxiety can have a big impact on your schooling, and consequently on your future.

Test anxiety can spread to other parts of your life. Anxiety on tests can become anxiety in any stressful situation, and blanking on a test can turn into panicking in a job situation. But fortunately, you don't have to let anxiety rule your testing and determine your grades. There are a number of relatively simple steps you can take to move past anxiety and function normally on a test and in the rest of life.

## Physical Steps for Beating Test Anxiety

While test anxiety is a serious problem, the good news is that it can be overcome. It doesn't have to control your ability to think and remember information. While it may take time, you can begin taking steps today to beat anxiety.

Just as your first hint that you may be struggling with anxiety comes from the physical symptoms, the first step to treating it is also physical. Rest is crucial for having a clear, strong mind. If you are tired, it is much easier to give in to anxiety. But if you establish good sleep habits, your body and mind will be ready to perform optimally, without the strain of exhaustion. Additionally, sleeping well helps you to retain information better, so you're more likely to recall the answers when you see the test questions.

Getting good sleep means more than going to bed on time. It's important to allow your brain time to relax. Take study breaks from time to time so it doesn't get overworked, and don't study right before bed. Take time to rest your mind before trying to rest your body, or you may find it difficult to fall asleep.

Along with sleep, other aspects of physical health are important in preparing for a test. Good nutrition is vital for good brain function. Sugary foods and drinks may give a burst of energy but this burst is followed by a crash, both physically and emotionally. Instead, fuel your body with protein and vitamin-rich foods.

Also, drink plenty of water. Dehydration can lead to headaches and exhaustion, especially if your brain is already under stress from the rigors of the test. Particularly if your test is a long one, drink water during the breaks. And if possible, take an energy-boosting snack to eat between sections.

Along with sleep and diet, a third important part of physical health is exercise. Maintaining a steady workout schedule is helpful, but even taking 5-minute study breaks to walk can help get your blood pumping faster and clear your head. Exercise also releases endorphins, which contribute to a positive feeling and can help combat test anxiety.

When you nurture your physical health, you are also contributing to your mental health. If your body is healthy, your mind is much more likely to be healthy as well. So take time to rest, nourish your body with healthy food and water, and get moving as much as possible. Taking these physical steps will make you stronger and more able to take the mental steps necessary to overcome test anxiety.

## Mental Steps for Beating Test Anxiety

Working on the mental side of test anxiety can be more challenging, but as with the physical side, there are clear steps you can take to overcome it. As mentioned earlier, test anxiety often stems from lack of preparation, so the obvious solution is to prepare for the test. Effective studying may be the most important weapon you have for beating test anxiety, but you can and should employ several other mental tools to combat fear.

First, boost your confidence by reminding yourself of past success—tests or projects that you aced. If you're putting as much effort into preparing for this test as you did for those, there's no reason you should expect to fail here. Work hard to prepare; then trust your preparation.

Second, surround yourself with encouraging people. It can be helpful to find a study group, but be sure that the people you're around will encourage a positive attitude. If you spend time with others who are anxious or cynical, this will only contribute to your own anxiety. Look for others who are motivated to study hard from a desire to succeed, not from a fear of failure.

Third, reward yourself. A test is physically and mentally tiring, even without anxiety, and it can be helpful to have something to look forward to. Plan an activity following the test, regardless of the outcome, such as going to a movie or getting ice cream.

When you are taking the test, if you find yourself beginning to feel anxious, remind yourself that you know the material. Visualize successfully completing the test. Then take a few deep, relaxing breaths and return to it. Work through the questions carefully but with confidence, knowing that you are capable of succeeding.

Developing a healthy mental approach to test taking will also aid in other areas of life. Test anxiety affects more than just the actual test—it can be damaging to your mental health and even contribute to depression. It's important to beat test anxiety before it becomes a problem for more than testing.

## Study Strategy

Being prepared for the test is necessary to combat anxiety, but what does being prepared look like? You may study for hours on end and still not feel prepared. What you need is a strategy for test prep. The next few pages outline our recommended steps to help you plan out and conquer the challenge of preparation.

### Step 1: Scope Out the Test

Learn everything you can about the format (multiple choice, essay, etc.) and what will be on the test. Gather any study materials, course outlines, or sample exams that may be available. Not only will this help you to prepare, but knowing what to expect can help to alleviate test anxiety.

### Step 2: Map Out the Material

Look through the textbook or study guide and make note of how many chapters or sections it has. Then divide these over the time you have. For example, if a book has 15 chapters and you have five days to study, you need to cover three chapters each day. Even better, if you have the time, leave an extra day at the end for overall review after you have gone through the material in depth.

If time is limited, you may need to prioritize the material. Look through it and make note of which sections you think you already have a good grasp on, and which need review. While you are studying, skim quickly through the familiar sections and take more time on the challenging parts.

Write out your plan so you don't get lost as you go. Having a written plan also helps you feel more in control of the study, so anxiety is less likely to arise from feeling overwhelmed at the amount to cover.

## Step 3: Gather Your Tools

Decide what study method works best for you. Do you prefer to highlight in the book as you study and then go back over the highlighted portions? Or do you type out notes of the important information? Or is it helpful to make flashcards that you can carry with you? Assemble the pens, index cards, highlighters, post-it notes, and any other materials you may need so you won't be distracted by getting up to find things while you study.

If you're having a hard time retaining the information or organizing your notes, experiment with different methods. For example, try color-coding by subject with colored pens, highlighters, or post-it notes. If you learn better by hearing, try recording yourself reading your notes so you can listen while in the car, working out, or simply sitting at your desk. Ask a friend to quiz you from your flashcards, or try teaching someone the material to solidify it in your mind.

## Step 4: Create Your Environment

It's important to avoid distractions while you study. This includes both the obvious distractions like visitors and the subtle distractions like an uncomfortable chair (or a too-comfortable couch that makes you want to fall asleep). Set up the best study environment possible: good lighting and a comfortable work area. If background music helps you focus, you may want to turn it on, but otherwise keep the room quiet. If you are using a computer to take notes, be sure you don't have any other windows open, especially applications like social media, games, or anything else that could distract you. Silence your phone and turn off notifications. Be sure to keep water close by so you stay hydrated while you study (but avoid unhealthy drinks and snacks).

Also, take into account the best time of day to study. Are you freshest first thing in the morning? Try to set aside some time then to work through the material. Is your mind clearer in the afternoon or evening? Schedule your study session then. Another method is to study at the same time of day that you will take the test, so that your brain gets used to working on the material at that time and will be ready to focus at test time.

## Step 5: Study!

Once you have done all the study preparation, it's time to settle into the actual studying. Sit down, take a few moments to settle your mind so you can focus, and begin to follow your study plan. Don't give in to distractions or let yourself procrastinate. This is your time to prepare so you'll be ready to fearlessly approach the test. Make the most of the time and stay focused.

Of course, you don't want to burn out. If you study too long you may find that you're not retaining the information very well. Take regular study breaks. For example, taking five minutes out of every hour to walk briskly, breathing deeply and swinging your arms, can help your mind stay fresh.

As you get to the end of each chapter or section, it's a good idea to do a quick review. Remind yourself of what you learned and work on any difficult parts. When you feel that you've mastered the material, move on to the next part. At the end of your study session, briefly skim through your notes again.

But while review is helpful, cramming last minute is NOT. If at all possible, work ahead so that you won't need to fit all your study into the last day. Cramming overloads your brain with more information than it can process and retain, and your tired mind may struggle to recall even previously learned information when it is overwhelmed with last-minute study. Also, the urgent nature of cramming and the stress placed on your brain contribute to anxiety. You'll be more likely to go to the test feeling unprepared and having trouble thinking clearly.

So don't cram, and don't stay up late before the test, even just to review your notes at a leisurely pace. Your brain needs rest more than it needs to go over the information again. In fact, plan to finish your studies by noon or early afternoon the day before the test. Give your brain the rest of the day to relax or focus on other things, and get a good night's sleep. Then you will be fresh for the test and better able to recall what you've studied.

### Step 6: Take a Practice Test

Many courses offer sample tests, either online or in the study materials. This is an excellent resource to check whether you have mastered the material, as well as to prepare for the test format and environment.

Check the test format ahead of time: the number of questions, the type (multiple choice, free response, etc.), and the time limit. Then create a plan for working through them. For example, if you have 30 minutes to take a 60-question test, your limit is 30 seconds per question. Spend less time on the questions you know well so that you can take more time on the difficult ones.

If you have time to take several practice tests, take the first one open book, with no time limit. Work through the questions at your own pace and make sure you fully understand them. Gradually work up to taking a test under test conditions: sit at a desk with all study materials put away and set a timer. Pace yourself to make sure you finish the test with time to spare and go back to check your answers if you have time.

After each test, check your answers. On the questions you missed, be sure you understand why you missed them. Did you misread the question (tests can use tricky wording)? Did you forget the information? Or was it something you hadn't learned? Go back and study any shaky areas that the practice tests reveal.

Taking these tests not only helps with your grade, but also aids in combating test anxiety. If you're already used to the test conditions, you're less likely to worry about it, and working through tests until you're scoring well gives you a confidence boost. Go through the practice tests until you feel comfortable, and then you can go into the test knowing that you're ready for it.

## Test Tips

On test day, you should be confident, knowing that you've prepared well and are ready to answer the questions. But aside from preparation, there are several test day strategies you can employ to maximize your performance.

First, as stated before, get a good night's sleep the night before the test (and for several nights before that, if possible). Go into the test with a fresh, alert mind rather than staying up late to study.

Try not to change too much about your normal routine on the day of the test. It's important to eat a nutritious breakfast, but if you normally don't eat breakfast at all, consider eating just a protein bar. If you're a coffee drinker, go ahead and have your normal coffee. Just make sure you time it so that the caffeine doesn't wear off right in the middle of your test. Avoid sugary beverages, and drink enough water to stay hydrated but not so much that you need a restroom break 10 minutes into the test. If your test isn't first thing in the morning, consider going for a walk or doing a light workout before the test to get your blood flowing.

Allow yourself enough time to get ready, and leave for the test with plenty of time to spare so you won't have the anxiety of scrambling to arrive in time. Another reason to be early is to select a good seat. It's helpful to sit away from doors and windows, which can be distracting. Find a good seat, get out your supplies, and settle your mind before the test begins.

When the test begins, start by going over the instructions carefully, even if you already know what to expect. Make sure you avoid any careless mistakes by following the directions.

Then begin working through the questions, pacing yourself as you've practiced. If you're not sure on an answer, don't spend too much time on it, and don't let it shake your confidence. Either skip it and come back later, or eliminate as many wrong answers as possible and guess among the remaining ones. Don't dwell on these questions as you continue—put them out of your mind and focus on what lies ahead.

Be sure to read all of the answer choices, even if you're sure the first one is the right answer. Sometimes you'll find a better one if you keep reading. But don't second-guess yourself if you do immediately know the answer. Your gut instinct is usually right. Don't let test anxiety rob you of the information you know.

If you have time at the end of the test (and if the test format allows), go back and review your answers. Be cautious about changing any, since your first instinct tends to be correct, but make sure you didn't misread any of the questions or accidentally mark the wrong answer choice. Look over any you skipped and make an educated guess.

At the end, leave the test feeling confident. You've done your best, so don't waste time worrying about your performance or wishing you could change anything. Instead, celebrate the successful completion of this test. And finally, use this test to learn how to deal with anxiety even better next time.

**Review Video: Test Anxiety**
Visit mometrix.com/academy and enter code: 100340

## Important Qualification

Not all anxiety is created equal. If your test anxiety is causing major issues in your life beyond the classroom or testing center, or if you are experiencing troubling physical symptoms related to your anxiety, it may be a sign of a serious physiological or psychological condition. If this sounds like your situation, we strongly encourage you to seek professional help.

## Online Resources

Due to our efforts to try to keep this book to a manageable length, we've created a link that will give you access to all of your online resources:

**mometrix.com/resources719/sspssag6ela**

# It's Your Moment, Let's Celebrate It!

Share your story @mometrixtestpreparation